SEP 8 5

DATE DUE	DATE DUE	DATE DUE	
APR 1 4 1987	JUN 3 0 1998		
AUG 0 4 1987	JUL 2 4 1998	APR 1 1 2001	
OCT 0 8 1987	JAN 2 2 1999		
NOV 0 5 198		OCT 1 2 2001	
DEC 0 7 198	JAN 2 2 1999	FEB 0 1 2002	
FEB 2 2 198	MAR 0 2 1999	MAR 0 6 2002	
MAR 2 1 198	MAR 1 5 1999		
APR 1 8 9	JUL 1 5 1999		
AUG 1 9 198	MAR 3 0 2000	APR 0 9 2002	
DEC 0 6 1988	MAY 2 4 2000	MAY 0 1 2002	
APR 2 0 198	APR 0 4 2001		
JUN 0 8 198		JUL 1 3 2002	

GAYLORD No. 2333   PRINTED IN U.S.A.

Diane M. Reed, an award-winning author/journalist for more than twenty years, married off two daughters "on a shoestring" using knowledge gained in more than a decade of reporting weddings as a society editor. She has written six books, has raised seven children, and today owns and operates United Marketing, a Long Beach, California, advertising agency.

the
"Oh, what a wonderful wedding"
book

Diane M. Reed

850797

Prentice-Hall, Inc., Englewood Cliffs, New Jersey 07632

Library of Congress Cataloging in Publication Data

Reed, Diane M.
  The "Oh, what a wonderful wedding" book.

  Rev. ed. of: The underground wedding book. 1973.
  Includes index.
  1. Weddings.   2. Finance, Personal.   I. Reed, Diane M.
The underground wedding book.   II. Title.
HQ745.R43 1984   395'.22   83-24724
ISBN 0-13-633421-0
ISBN 0-13-633413-X (pbk.)

This book is available at a special discount when ordered in bulk quantities. Contact Prentice-Hall, Inc., General Publishing Division, Special Sales, Englewood Cliffs, N.J. 07632.

Previously published as *The Underground Wedding Book* by Price/Stern/Sloan.
Copyright © 1973 by Diane Reed.
Illustrations copyright © 1973 by Price/Stern/Sloan.

10 9 8 7 6 5 4 3 2 1

ISBN 0-13-633421-0

ISBN 0-13-633413-X {PBK.}

Editorial/production supervision by Norma G. Ledbetter
Cover design by Hal Siegel
Illustrations by Dianne Birnbaum
Manufacturing buyer: Pat Mahoney

PRENTICE-HALL INTERNATIONAL, INC., *London*
PRENTICE-HALL OF AUSTRALIA PTY. LIMITED, *Sydney*
PRENTICE-HALL CANADA INC., *Toronto*
PRENTICE-HALL OF INDIA PRIVATE LIMITED, *New Delhi*
PRENTICE-HALL OF JAPAN, INC., *Tokyo*
PRENTICE-HALL OF SOUTHEAST ASIA PTE. LTD., *Singapore*
WHITEHALL BOOKS LIMITED, *Wellington, New Zealand*
EDITORA PRENTICE-HALL DO BRASIL LTDA., *Rio de Janeiro*

*This book is dedicated with love
to my adorable daughter Holly, who at 12 often spent
her allowance at the florist, buying roses one at a time
to encourage me as I labored over my first book.*

*I have watched you blossom into a beautiful woman,
a graceful rose, worthy of any wedding bouquet,
through the many years and books since quarters could
buy roses. And, it has been a delight.*

*I dedicate this book to you with gratitude, not only
for becoming the kind of daughter every mother dreams of,
but for intrinsically understanding the creative process
and a mother who wrote books while other mothers
were reading them to their little girls.*

*This book is truly yours, Holly, for it is
both serious and funny, loving and light-hearted,
full of hope and unexpected surprises,
just as you are.*

*I look forward to your wedding day,
knowing that you will be the most beautiful of brides
and confident that you will be
a wonderful wife as well.*
Mom

contents

preface

Romance knows no timetable. Weddings seldom take place when families can best afford them. I found this out firsthand, when my adopted daughter Nancy announced her engagement the day after I had spent my life savings on a dream house by the sea! Her sister Susan waited a while—she chose the week the second mortgage was due to announce her wedding plans!

But both girls, with willing hands and warm hearts, let love and not money make their weddings cherished memories for everyone involved.

If you are a woman whose wedding dreams are bigger by far than her budget, this book will show you how to have the wedding you want at a price you can afford.

No matter how small your budget is, you can't afford *not* to buy and read The *"Oh, What a Wonderful Wedding" Book*.

If you use just one money-saving idea from the bridal bounty inside, you will recover the purchase price. And if you grasp the creative approach to life that is a free bonus here, you will find a wealth of wisdom that can make you not only a beautiful bride but a warm and wonderful wife as well.

If you can afford the best that money can buy but are one of those rare young women in that financial bracket who want a wedding that is more than "just a pretty face," you, too, will find a treasure trove of ideas here. Within these pages are ideas guaranteed to put your wedding in a class by itself!

Representing the expertise gained during a decade of daily association with engaged girls, brides, and their mothers, this is the only book dedicated to showing you in detail how to give your wedding the kind of million-dollar dazzle that no amount of money can buy.

Buy the book now, and carry it with you as you consummate your wedding plans. If you use it as it is intended to be used, you'll find it not only a source of inspiration but a useful handbook that will become a daily guide from your engagement through your wedding day, and a treasured memento forever.

This is a book to share with your mother now and with your daughters in years to come. It is a book to give to friends when they announce their engagements and one whose title will ring in your ears at your reception.

Listen carefully, after you use it. You'll hear your guests repeating time and again, "Oh, What a Wonderful Wedding!"

introduction

As a society editor, working with engaged women and reporting their weddings for more than ten years, I have found more and more that money is far from the most important factor in putting together a wedding that will be warmly remembered. Enthusiasm, creativity, warmth, and a sentimentally romantic approach rank far ahead of finance in leaving a lasting impression.

How to put these qualities to work to make your wedding sparkle with a stamp that marks it "very truly yours" is the essence of this book. Drawing on the successes and failures of thousands of brides, it gives you the benefit of their most creative moments and most successful money-saving ideas. The kinds of dreams that came true for these women—who let love take over when the money ran out—can come true for you, too. That's why this book is a must, whether you are getting married next month or have only just begun to zero in on the mate of your choice.

This book offers ideas and information that will make it possible for you to have the kind of wedding you have always wanted without fear of putting your parents or yourself in the poorhouse. This is the book that mass merchandisers of wedding wares hoped would never be written. Exploding the myth that beautiful weddings are always budget breakers, this handbook for the bride-to-be offers a bounty of alternatives to the costly wedding packages highly touted by bridal consultants nationwide.

With a nostalgic feeling of bygone days—when weddings, like funerals and christenings, were occasions for family and friends to pool their talents and give lovingly of their time—the book revives the romance of one-of-a-kind weddings, handwrought with love for a perfectly wonderful way to go from single woman to wife.

With the "now" notion that if your budget won't stretch, then your mind must, it invites you to do the unconventional, to look in new directions and explore alternatives in all phases of wedding planning. And if you think your mind won't stretch, this book will prove you wrong.

Providing you with ideas so delightful and innovative, so valuable and inexpensive that you'll find it hard to choose between them, it will start a chain reaction that is guaranteed to make your wedding not only as good as your bank balance will allow, but better than any amount of money could buy.

1
dreams and themes
are free

The happy sound of wedding bells doesn't have to be drowned out by the constant ringing of cash registers.

You can be a beautiful bride with more love than money and have a wedding that will be warmly remembered by everyone involved, even the person who pays the bills.

Brides today have more freedom in making wedding plans than ever before, and creative women are using this new-found freedom to make their weddings more meaningful and less expensive whenever possible.

The first step to a wedding that is uniquely yours and uncommonly inexpensive is selecting a theme. Themes, like dreams, are free. So dream big to begin with, then scale those dreams down to budget size, keeping the essence as your theme.

If you have always wanted a wedding rich in Old World charm, or one with an exotic island influence, now is the time to say so. Far from increasing the cost of your wedding, selecting a theme and sticking to it can provide a multitude of delightful "excuses" for cutting costs—and the inspiration for doing so, as well.

Themes can be carried to varying extremes, from just a hint of the romance of a bygone era to an authentic ethnic festival. The choice is yours, but whatever you select, let it set the mood for the entire affair from site to attire and menu to music.

Themes can be found in many ways, in recollections of a first meeting, in shared interests, family heritages, honeymoon plans, or in nostalgia for another era. They can be subtle or bold, but most often they reflect the personalities of the bride and groom.

Almost all weddings have themes, whether or not the couples realize it. Even the most traditional weddings—the white-on-white, lace-on-satin variety—can be grouped into categories such as Colonial, Victorian, Renaissance-look, peasant and the like.

Find Excuses to Save

Often, selecting an unusual theme can be a brilliant opportunity for cutting costs while coming up with a wedding that will be a glowing memory for a price that would be just a glimmer for a traditionally styled wedding.

4

The point is, don't be walled in by tradition if you don't want to be.

One of the most impressive weddings I ever reported was a ceremony linking two Peace Corps volunteers, both of Irish ancestry. They selected an African motif for their wedding because they had met in Kenya and fallen in love with each other, as well as the customs of the Dark Continent, while on assignment there.

The bride selected a colorful African gown for her wedding, one made of hand-printed fabric she'd brought home from her mission store. The bridesmaids dressed similarly and carried baskets of flowers on their heads (after much practice) instead of carrying nosegays. The ushers carried drums and donned flowing robes, like the one worn by the groom, making a striking and unforgettable picture for wedding guests—who each carried home a copy of the wedding ceremony translated into Swahili as an added remembrance of the event.

The bride's mother confided, sometime later, that while she had been against the idea in the beginning, she had been thrilled by the response of wedding guests who felt the deep meaning the unique ceremony had for the couple. She added that the bride's father had been pleasantly surprised, too, particularly when the final bills were in. These truly memorable rites had cost considerably less than he had estimated spending for a smaller, more traditional ritual.

Ethnic Weddings Popular

Ethnic weddings, while not always as unconventional as this one, are becoming extremely popular with young couples. In Black, Mexican-American, and Oriental homes where family culture is stressed today, more and more brides are selecting wedding ceremonies that reflect their colorful ancestry.

Many Anglo brides are borrowing the color and charm of such rites for their own wedding days or delving into their family histories for other ideas.

There are many inexpensive themes that are both romantic and impressive. Here are a dozen to consider before making your final plans.

The Heirloom Wedding. This is a sentimental ceremony that relies on treasured hand-me-downs to cut costs while building romanticism.

The Peasant Wedding. An ideal, informal ceremony can be held outdoors in a meadow or at the seashore. A young "now" ceremony supremely suited to an inexpensive picnic-style reception.

The Hawaiian Wedding. A colorful, romantic, exotic island motif and luau reception can be as moving as the strains of the Hawaiian Wedding Song.

The Victorian Wedding. As pretty as a valentine of red satin and paper lace, and just as charming, this is the perfect ceremony for reciting sonnets or having harpsichord music, if that's your thing.

The Acapulco Wedding. Here is an ethnic-style ceremony that is bright and gay in every way. And lucky the people in areas near Old Mexico, for they will find perfect settings, props and cos-

6

tumes at hand to help stage such a wedding beautifully, at a fraction of what it would cost elsewhere.

The Pioneer Wedding. This would be great for DAR-types and proud pilgrims. You can wear a pinafore and a poke bonnet and have a hayride or barn dance reception. What fun!

The Afro Wedding. Call on the color and ritual of African ancestry to make it a meaningful expression of why you think black really is beautiful.

The Camelot Wedding. Be enchanting as a fairy tale. You are the queen and he's your shining knight, and you'll reign over a regal reception, together.

Rock 'n' Roll Wedding. Up-beat and oh, so young, the Rock 'n' Roll wedding may be "punk," "fifties," "new wave," "rock-a-billy," or the hard stuff, and still be romantic and fun. Let the music be the theme and "roll-out" from there, with appropriate costumes

"CAMELOT"

and catering. This theme is best done outdoors and far from complaining neighbors, however!

The Oriental Wedding. Steeped in tradition, elegant in its simplicity, this is fabulous in a well-manicured garden where the reception follows right on the spot.

The Thirties-Look Wedding. Sexy you, in slinky satin with yards and yards of veil. Nostaligic you, recalling memories of movie queens past.

The American Indian Wedding. Buckskin and beads, a ceremonial fire, a gown you can make at home without a sewing machine—all this is ideal for the all-American woman.

Depending on your family background, interests, honeymoon destination, and the like, you may have a dozen more to add to the list, or none of these may strike your fancy. A word of caution here, however. If none of the themes that come to mind really excites you, try "something old, something new, something borrowed, something blue" and leave it at that. Don't run the risk of turning your ceremony from spectacular into a spectacle, just trying to make it unique.

Do Your Thing Enthusiastically

If, on the other hand, you have always wanted to do something really far out on your wedding day, like saying your vows in the bowling alley where you met (and in spite of tradition, anything else would seem like second best), do it! But don't spring it on wedding guests at the last moment, or the surprise might come more as a shock.

Whatever your theme, whisper it to friends from the start so that they have an opportunity to catch your enthusiasm for it. Let them enjoy a period of anticipation in advance of the "grand occasion" rather than a moment of shock when the address on the wed-

PASS ENTHUSIASM FOR THE THEME
TO THE EXPECTED GUESTS ...AND GROOM!

ding invitation turns out to be a family bowling center instead of a church.

If you can't be so enthusiastic about your wedding theme that no one could doubt its meaning for you—better think twice about using it.

A good test of a workable theme is whether or not it is easy for you to discuss it enthusiastically with friends. Start with your fiancé. After all, without him you wouldn't be planning a wedding, so don't make up your mind to anything without getting his view of the idea, too.

Many of the popular ethnic themes and a few of the traditional ones—the Victorian, the Camelot, or the Pioneer, for example—afford an opportunity for the groom to have a wedding costume that is something more than just a rented tuxedo.

If your fiancé is as enthusiastic about the theme you select as you are, he can participate in making it come alive by dressing to the occasion and helping coordinate other facets of the wedding to carry out the theme more fully.

Like the young Peace Corps volunteers, yours can be a wedding with a truly "total look" if you enlist the aid of the male members of the wedding party as well as the females in making this dream come true. In addition to dressing the part, the men in your wedding party can add a great deal to the occasion by making certain that such items as music and transportation are in keeping with the theme, too.

A delightful example of what can be done to make a wedding dream come true was the Pioneer wedding of a pair of youngsters who had been labeled "punkers" by their family and older acquaintances, as so many youngsters are today.

Set in a rustic chapel in a Seattle suburb, that wedding was a revelation to the over-40 crowd. It was as if the clock had been turned back to a place in time where the long-haired young men with their mutton-chop sideburns and beards were The Establishment crowd, and the clean-shaven gentlemen with their Sunday shirts on were the ones out of step with the crowd.

Wearing calico dresses and poke bonnets they had made themselves, the women were nothing less than smashing. In Western clothes—Levis with open-collared shirts of matching calico prints—the young men in the wedding party were as relaxed and comfortable as they were good looking.

The ceremony, which featured folk music of the period played and sung by members of the wedding party, was much more a celebration than a solemn rite. It was a revealing look at what the youthful participants really thought a wedding should be, and no one argued with their point of view.

This wedding was fun, festive and markedly meaningful, from the handmade costumes to the seemingly spontaneous vows the bride and groom exchanged in their own words.

It was so romantic, so utterly charming in its simplicity, that, even before the "parson" pronounced the couple husband and wife, guests were certain this was a love story destined to have a happy ending.

The wedding, however, was only the beginning. As guests left the church, they were taken, a few at a time, by hay wagon to a clearing in the woods nearby to enjoy a pioneer-style reception complete with hootenanny, barn dancing and a pot-luck supper.

In less than an hour not a man in the place was wearing a tie, and before the afternoon event was over, nearly everyone had heard his or her favorite song played on the guitars that were in abundance, or had a chance to dance with the bride or groom.

When it came time for the young couple to depart, the hay wagon was again pressed into service, and trailing old shoes, pots, and pans, it drove them back to the church, with wedding guests following on foot, singing, laughing, and shouting in shivaree-style as they made their way to their cars.

For all the old-fashioned fun of the festive event, it might have cost a million. The bride's father still boasts, however, that in spite of a wedding party of 12 and more than 100 guests who ate, drank, and danced to their hearts' content, the whole affair cost him less than $500.

How? They did it with love—and so can you!

2
ten commandments for the budget-minded bride

1. THOU SHALT NOT ENTER ANY BRIDAL BOUTIQUE
WITH CASH, CHECKBOOK, OR CREDIT CARDS IN THY
POSSESSION.

Every bride enjoys shopping for the beautiful things that will make
her wedding day a dream come true. But smart women carry a
notebook, not a checkbook. And they leave cash and credit cards in
the custody of a frugal friend!

With this minor bit of preparation you can go on a shopping
spree to the most expensive boutiques in town and shop as if money
were no object, for you'll be spying, not buying.

With a sharp eye, a sharp pencil, and a small investment of
time, you can have anything you find in these boutiques at pennies
on the dollar.

First make lists—lots of lists. Jot down every item you find
that you would really like to have for your wedding.

But don't stop there. List the fabrics, colors, sizes, manufacturers, prices, and any other information you can glean from the salesperson who waits on you. Advice is free, and you might as well get it
from the experts!

Even if your artistic talent is confined to "paint-by-numbers,"
make small sketches of the things that really catch your eye. That

way you won't confuse the cerise satin with the red taffeta gown when you go over your notes.

And when you compare prices or seek substitutes for these costly items later, you'll have everything that you need in black and white.

2. THOU SHALT NOT BUY ON IMPULSE!

Mass merchandisers of wedding wares rely on impulse and emotion to make their astounding profits. So be strong! No matter how much you'd like to buy, confine your shopping expeditions to looking instead, and look carefully.

Never buy anything that you haven't gotten at least three prices on. And never, Never, NEVER be swayed by a salesperson who tells you that a store is the only one that carries a particular item, or that what you fancy is the last one within a hundred miles.

So-called wedding "consultants" are nothing more than super salespeople, and they know that this is your most vulnerable shoping time.

3. THOU SHALT NEVER BUY WHAT THOU CANST BORROW, RENT, OR MAKE!

As you shop, consider alternatives for every item you find attractive. If you like a headpiece that looks like a derby with a dashing splash of veil, look it over with an eye to how you can purchase an inexpensive hat of the same shape and add some inexpensive tulle or blusher to it to achieve the same effect.

If you fancy a lavish champagne fountain for your reception but the price tag is larger than your entire wedding budget, sketch it and then take your sketches to a party rental shop and see how much you'll save by renting one for the day.

If the $200 shoes your sorority sister wore at her wedding are the only ones you've seen that would be perfect with your gown, find out what size they are; and if you can wear them, ask to borrow them for your big day.

DECORATED PRAYER BOOK
WITH ONE FLOWER!

4. THOU SHALT ALWAYS SEEK A DUAL PURPOSE FOR
   ITEMS PURCHASED.

This is particularly true of the purchases you must make to decorate the church and reception place.

Don't buy items that will only be used for one or the other.
And, don't buy anything that will be useless later!

If you must have satin pew bows for the church, buy or make
them to do double duty as decorations for the reception as well.
While you're posing for pictures after the ceremony, have your attendants whisk them into the reception hall and festoon the buffet
table, entrance, or bandstand with them before the reception starts.

If you simply have to have bowers of flowers on the altar, rather than buying two or three huge sprays, opt for several smaller
baskets on pedestals—the baskets can adorn the cake table, the
beverage bar, or the gift display table later.

If the gown you select for yourself (or those you choose for
your attendants) will only fit your mental image of "perfect" if it
has a train ten yards long, make it a detachable train so that you
and your attendants can "recycle" the dresses for other occasions.

If you want baskets or candles or bud vases for each table at
the reception, instead of buying two dozen exactly alike that you'll
have no use for later, consider buying two or three of several different kinds so that when you take them home, you can use them in
pairs or mix them for interesting groupings in your apartment or

14

house. Two or three of a kind will be ample for each table, and useful later on. Twenty-four identical bud vases are more than a lifetime supply.

One smart bride I know who used white wicker baskets for her reception tables made certain that each was a different shape and size and later used them as a striking wall treatment in her dining room, above a white wicker table and chairs.

5. THOU SHALT COPY WHAT THOU CANST NOT AFFORD!

The day after Lady Diana became Princess to Charles of England, bridal shops around the globe began offering copies of her royal wedding dress. And eager brides snapped them up by the gross.

There is nothing wrong with copying what you cannot afford. And if you can't do it yourself, there are lots of people who can.

If you see a divine dress that is way out of your price bracket, get the best picture of it possible. Leaf through the bridal magazines, comb the catalogs, or be bold and brash and take your Polaroid right into the shop and snap it from every angle. Tell the salesperson that you're considering it but have to send snaps to Mom, miles away, for her opinion before you buy. Tell the salesperson anything you like. But get the pictures.

Then you have several options. If you sew, take the photos to the fabric shop and seek a similar fabric and pattern and start stitching until you have a duplicate.

If you don't sew, find a seamstress and seek her or his help. Or, if you live in a large city, go down to the garment district and, armed with your photos, see what you can find that is available at wholesale that is close and have it altered to match.

This idea doesn't have to be confined to clothing either. You can photograph flower arrangements, rings, cakes, and so on and "knock them off" at substantial savings. And no one will be the wiser, unless you share the secret.

I have a friend, married a year ago, who selected her gown from a Rodeo Drive boutique in Beverly Hills. She got a helpful salesperson to let her take it out on the condition that she could return it in twenty-four hours if her fiancé didn't like it for any reason. She then went directly to the downtown Los Angeles garment district and found a tailor who photographed it from neckline to hem, and she returned it—no questions asked.

On her wedding day, she stepped down the aisle looking like she'd just stepped out of the window on Rodeo Drive, but the dress the boutique had asked $1,750 for was hers for $57.75 cash, and I'll bet the designer couldn't have told the difference between the two.

6. THOU SHALT NOT HIRE A HALL WHEN FREE SPACE IS AVAILABLE.

The second largest expense most brides encounter is the price of a hall in which to hold their receptions. Hotel ballrooms, country club dining rooms, and yes, even church reception halls, can be extremely expensive. But there are alternatives.

Why spend hundreds of dollars just for "space" when there are all kinds of public meeting rooms, auditoriums, amphitheaters, and the like available at low or no cost.

Once you decide how many guests you will be entertaining, comb your community for possible locations for your reception that won't cost you an arm and a leg. If you will be married in the spring or summer, consider a park or beach, a picnic area or school auditorium. Dare to be different! A party is not a place; it is an atmosphere you can create. And it can be just as much fun and just as elegant in an inexpensive or free room as in the best restaurant in town. In fact, it may be even more so. For, if you spend less on the site, you'll have more to spend on food and beverages, a band, or the towering cake you long for.

7. THOU SHALT SHUN PROFESSIONAL CATERERS LIKE THE PLAGUE.

Catered, sit-down dinners and buffets are a costly portion of any wedding tab. And caterers are in business to make money, not to help penny-wise brides like you.

To avoid getting caught in the sales web of these greedy cooks in chic clothing, stay out of their establishments altogether.

Instead, let your fingers do the walking, and keep them at a respectable distance, by phone.

Why should you call a caterer if you aren't going to use one? Silly girl . . . to pump them for information, of course!

If you know of caterers in town, and they don't know you, call them and give them your ideas for your reception—how many you'll be serving, whether you plan a buffet, full meal, just cake and punch, or something in between. Ask for suggestions as to menus, presentation of the food, linens, and so on. And ask for prices.

Take copious notes. Find out what they serve for $2 per person, $10 per person, $20, and yes, even $50 per person. Then review these suggestions and go to the market, bakery, and so on and see how much of what they have to offer you can obtain for the price that best fits your budget. You'll be surprised how much farther your money will go.

And, once you've decided what and how much to serve, then shop where they shop—at wholesale grocery stores that supply restaurants, hotels, and the like.

You'll be amazed to find that such outlets carry economy-sized cans, boxes, and tubs of goodies that can often go directly to the table with little or no cooking. You'll find heat-and-serve casseroles, ready-stuffed game hens, boned turkey and chicken, marinated mushrooms and artichoke hearts, and much, much more at 10 to 25% of what the caterer would charge to open the cans and boxes for you. Look them up in the Yellow Pages!

8. THOU SHALT NOT BE INTIMIDATED BY "TRADITION."

Tradition is one of those words that are used to manipulate people into thinking that they *must* do something just because everyone has done it that way for years. It is also one of those words that puts an immediate damper on creativity.

So, even if you are planning what you believe to be a very traditional ceremony, don't be persuaded to buy or do anything you don't really want to just because someone tries to tell you that is the traditional way.

In today's culture virtually anything goes. And there is nothing nicer than to start your own "tradition" by doing something that will save you money and satisfy your desire to be unique in the bargain.

If you want to sing at your own wedding, rather than hiring a soloist, *sing!* (And save the soloist's fee for the rental on your honeymoon suite.)

If you just know your "guest book" is going to wind up gathering dust in your closet after you pay an arm and leg for it, but you want a record of everyone who was at the wedding, have guests sign a luncheon cloth spread atop a table just before they enter the receiving line and later embroider over their signatures, for an everlasting memento of the occasion that you can trot out for anniversary dinners throughout your married life.

If you can't stand the idea of paying more for your photo album than for the photographs inside it, purchase an inexpensive album and cover it with fabric and ribbon scraps from your wedding gown (see Bouquet of Beautiful Ideas for directions). You'll have a book that will give your children a chance not only to see how you looked on your wedding day, but also to touch and feel the satin of your gown and the lace that was on it.

9. WASTE NOT, WANT NOT!

Use everything you buy. That seems like just common sense, but you'd be surprised at how many brides buy more than they need of so many things.

A little time spent with a calculator (a great job for your husband-to-be) can do wonders in keeping the bridal budget in check.

Don't guess how many paper plates, napkins, book matches, and yards of streamers you will need. Have him figure it out *before* you go the store!

And if you are making your gowns or having them made, keep the scraps and put them to good use! Scraps from the bride's gown are always ample enough to make a pillow for the ring bearer, to cover a headpiece, to trim flower baskets, to add appliqués to fabric shoes, to use as mats inside wedding picture frames, and so on.

Scraps from the bridesmaid's gowns are perfect for trimming picture hats, making bows for their bouquets, or for making sentimental toss pillows for the bridal bedroom.

Extra babies' breath or other flowers can be used to enhance the presentation of food at the reception—to garnish meat platters, to ring serving dishes, to top the cake, or even to float in the punch bowl. These are things that caterers do all the time and charge you like sin for!

10. THOU SHALT KEEP THE FAITH NO MATTER WHAT!

No matter how meager your resources seem, you can have a wonderful wedding. And you don't have to hock your mother's jewels to do it.

Have faith in your own abilities. Have faith in your friends. Have faith in your creativity. Have faith in your dream, and dream out loud.

Those who love you will want your day to be everything you've ever dreamed of. Your enthusiasm and faith that the wedding of your childhood dreams can become a reality will go a long way toward making it happen.

So don't despair. Share! Don't hesitate to ask for help. A wedding is a wonderful, exciting occasion. And the more of your friends and relatives you involve in the actual planning and preparations, the more delightful your day will be.

Just think how happy Aunt Ruth will be to see you wearing her diamond earrings as your something borrowed. And imagine how pleased cousin Jill will be to hear guests ooohing and aaahing over the flowers she has arranged (and maybe even grown).

And consider how proud your future mother-in-law will be that you asked her to ice your cake because she's the best baker in town.

Be a "Daydream Believer," and the day you've dreamed of will be better than you've ever thought possible—believe me!

3
to church
or not to church

Once you have selected a theme and a tentative date for your wedding, you are ready to explore the available sites.

If you are a regular churchgoer, you will probably want to be married in the church you attend each Sunday, but if not, don't feel obligated to do so. "To church or not to church?" is a serious question and one that should be considered carefully before any decision is made.

If the kind of wedding you have selected cries out for a formal religious ceremony, your choice will be a relatively routine one. If, on the other hand, you favor less formal or even, nonreligious rites, you will want to consider a variety of settings. Some weddings are supremely suited to an intimate home setting; others demand the formality of a religious backdrop; and still others demand something really different.

Do Something Spectacular

A couple I recall, who met and fell in love during a summer vacation at Lake Tahoe, on the California-Nevada border, decided to hold their unique wedding at the water's edge in the spectacular natural setting that had provided the inspiration for their romance. Their fabulous wedding gathered 400 guests at the lakeside for an impressive ceremony in which the minister spoke eloquently of the creation of man and woman and God's hope for them as ideal mates. In the awe-inspiring natural atmosphere of the High Sierra setting, guests came away feeling that they, as human beings, were a part of the beauty they had witnessed and not simply intruders in a spot so beautiful it seemed almost sacred.

You can leave guests with a lasting impression of your wedding in many ways, but the place in which you recite your vows will always be an integral part of their memories of the event.

There are many places other than churches and synagogues to say your wedding vows. Of course there are the obvious: campus and military chapels, the costly hotels and private clubs, and the freaky sites that make headlines, like underwater or in a balloon or inside the Statue of Liberty. But if none of these seems desirable to you, don't despair.

Explore All Possible Sites

The next time you and your fiancé have nothing to do, jump in the car or on a bike or a bus and take a leisurely tour of your favorite spots around town. Make a list as you go, jotting down possible spots for your wedding and reception. Let your imaginations fly, noting any place along the way that strikes your fancy, from Central Park to the local movie house or concert hall. You'll be surprised what splendid settings there are in unexpected places.

BOWLING ALLEY

Every town of any size has a funeral home, for example, but before you exclude the chapel located there, stop by and talk to the mortuary director. She or he will be happy to show you the facilities, and you may be delighted by how beautifully serene the chapel is. It may also surprise you to find out that these chapels are often offered free for weddings as a community service. Whatever the case, it doesn't cost anything to do some comparative shopping for a site, just as you would for any other item on your wedding list.

In case you are squeamish about the thought of a mortuary chapel, let me say that my own daughter was married in one, an intimate chapel of glass and rock set in a garden of lush green splendor and furnished with antiques of the Victorian era (which she had chosen as the theme for her wedding). Nothing could have been more beautiful, if I do say so myself, and I certainly wasn't the only one who commented on it.

Once you have completed your list of possible sites, review it with care, adding to it notes or questions you might have about the facilities, the costs, and possibility of holding a wedding there. Then turn to the telephone book and look up numbers to call in order to get answers to your questions.

In selecting a location for your wedding, the key to keeping costs low and impact high is a little creative thought. When you think you have run out of ideas, run down the family and wedding party roster, listing all the organizations to which members belong. The local woman's club, lodge, service club, Boy's Club, YMCA, and union hall are all possible spots. Most have facilities for large meetings, and some will be equipped with kitchen and bar, perfect for an on-the-spot reception. Many communities also have recreation halls, park buildings, teen centers, or other meeting places that are made available nights and weekends as a public service, either free or at a very nominal fee.

Screen Them Carefully

Once your list of such sites is complete, set aside a time to explore each item on it further by phone. Make it a quiet morning when you have time to chat. Supply yourself with a steno pad or tablet, pencils, and a calendar. Begin by making another list—this one's easy—of questions that will get you the answers you need quickly and without wasting too much of your time or the time of those you will be calling.

A sample list might be:

1. Would it be possible to hold a wedding in your facility?
2. If so, would there be a fee and how much?
3. What are the rules?
4. Are there kitchen or bar facilities?
5. What dates are open?
6. What hours?
7. How far in advance must reservations be made?

With a list like this you won't waste time asking about kitchens, seating capacity, and the like when there is a strict rule against weddings, and you won't be embarrassed by extreme cost after having exclaimed over "perfect" facilities which you may not be able to afford.

Find Out About Food

If you plan to cater the reception yourself, you will want to add questions regarding the regulations governing this to your list:

1. Do you have linens or table service available?
2. Will I have to provide my own punch bowl.?
3. Is alcohol allowed on the premises? Will there be a corkage fee?
4. Is a clean-up deposit or professional janitor required?

Many free facilities have rules against liquor (particularly public halls). Many lodges that offer both kitchen and bar facilities will allow you to do your own catering but will tack on a corkage or service charge that can run up the tab—immeasurably if you do not use their personnel or catering service.

It is best to find out all of this in the beginning, before you decide on a site. Nothing would be worse than having invitations printed and having to change the site because it became economically unfeasible after they were ordered.

If you decide on a site outdoors (other than in the family garden or churchyard), make certain you have the exact address of the site—and if that doesn't consist of street numbers or something similarly easy to decipher, include a map with the invitation. Your dream setting, that sunlit glen or oceanfront cove, may be just the location that will make your wedding the superspectacular event you want it to be—but what if you gave a wedding and nobody came?

Home Weddings

Home weddings are being revived with the sudden surge of nostalgia for other eras. And although it is true that they haven't reached the peak of popularity they enjoyed during World War II (when they were in vogue mainly because other sites were unavailable on short notice), home weddings are high on the list of site priorities for many brides.

Today, being married at home is usually by choice rather than necessity. Many young women, from the time they are tiny tots, dream of stepping down the family stairs in their wedding gowns. Others have always wanted to be married in front of the fireplace where they hung their stocking each Christmas as a child, and there are those who want to wed under the tall tree that was just a twig in childhood days. To still other girls, a home wedding is a particular salute to their mothers, a final thank-you to mom for years of making the house a home.

Whatever the reason, a home wedding should be considered, whether the house is a cottage or a mansion. Among the advantages of a home ceremony are: decorations do double duty, serving both wedding and reception; the atmosphere is rich in memories for the bride; there will be no problem transporting food, decorations or gown to a distant site; and of course the price is right!

Take a good look at the family home. Consider the accommodations there with a critical eye, looking not only for available space to seat guests but for settings both inside and out that would provide a romantic backdrop suitable for reciting your vows.

If the living room is too small, consider a family room, basement playroom, or den. If none of these seem right, a patio or garden sun deck or balcony might solve the problem, serving as a stage for the rites while guests view the ceremony from an adjacent room or outdoor area.

A home wedding I attended as a child has remained vividly in my memory ever since, because of the unique staging of the ceremony. Guests were seated in a backyard garden facing the house—a large old California Spanish-style residence—with a rear balcony outside the master bedroom upstairs. The organist played in the garden, and as the music of "The Wedding March" began and guests started to look for the wedding party, a pair of bridesmaids emerged from opposite sides of the house and stepped to either side of the balcony. Each took hold of a wide ribbon attached to the French doors, and as they pulled, the doors were opened and the bride and her father appeared, followed by the judge who performed the ceremony, the best man, and the groom.

It wasn't a very large balcony, just about big enough for the principals in the wedding, but for the guests seated in the garden below, watching the couple recite their vows from that flower-trimmed platform was an unforgettable experience.

Consider This

The point, here, is before you cross your home off your list of possible sites, do a little mental gymnastics and really look at every possibility at home. You can do a lot of decorating, fixing up, and advance preparations there with the money you might otherwise spend on renting a hall, chapel, or hotel for the rites. And you can do them at your leisure, little by little, without worrying about transporting decorations, food, or the like at the last minute.

If your home is just not an appealing site, or simply won't accommodate the number of guests you plan to receive, here are some tips in selecting another location from the bounty of bridal settings available in every town.

Try This Test

Ask yourself these questions:

1. Does the site have the look you are trying to achieve?
2. Is it free? Or does the fee involved seem within your reach?
3. Will it comfortably accommodate your guests?
4. Will they be pleasantly surprised at the setting you have selected?
5. Is it easy to find?
6. Will you be able to hold the reception there as well?
7. Is parking a problem?
8. Is weather a problem?
9. Is there a kitchen? A bar?
10. Will you be proud to invite your friends there?

If the answer to all or most of these questions is yes, you have a winning location for your special day. If not, either try the test on another site or explore the problems of this site and see if they can be worked out.

Some Solutions

Suppose the site looks perfect, is priced right, and will comfortably accommodate your guests but is difficult to find and has either a limited amount of parking or none at all within a block's distance? You may want to direct guests to an easy-to-find-and-park location nearby, and provide a shuttle service, letting the ushers caravan guests to the site in decorated "limousines." This will be a touch that is guaranteed to leave a lasting impression and will turn the problem of such a site into a plus.

What else could happen? Perhaps the location you just love has no kitchen facilities or reception hall and, because of fickle weather, would not be suitable for an outdoor reception. You could take your second choice and always feel that it was second best or pinch your pennies on other portions of the wedding and splurge on rented canvas awnings or tents to provide shelter and a pretty backdrop outside, then plan reception food that is prepared in advance and easily transportable.

What if you will not feel confident about inviting your guests to such an unusual setting (a theater or concert hall, for example) even though it may have all the other attributes you desire in a wedding and reception site? You can throw up your hands and cry or put your imagination to work on ways to make the setting more attractive.

If it's a theater, for example, you might create invitations that invite guests to "Our Love Story" and select the theme from the motion picture for the music. Or you could select a memorable line from a favorite motion picture love story to include in your vows, such as "Love means never having to say you're sorry," or perhaps a whole speech from a film or play. If you made up your own, could you do better than Shakespeare?

If the location you rate number one on your "perfect setting" list has problems other than these, play the "What Can Go Wrong?" game with your fiancé, mother, bridesmaids, and anyone else who will listen, until you find solutions that either turn the problems into assets, or at least make molehills out of what may have seemed insurmountable mountains at first glance.

To church or not to church?—that is the question, and the choice is up to you.

4
guest list

In order to keep costs of your wedding and reception to a minimum, you will want to keep close track of your wedding guest list. This is especially important if you are planning a full meal at the reception. Food for even a dozen extra people can cost a great deal. And, not enough food can cost even more in terms of embarrassment.

On the following pages, you will find a chart for entering the names of guests with places to check them off as they accept or send their regrets, the number who will attend in each party, and whether they will attend both the wedding and reception, or just one or the other.

If you take time now to enter the names of all you plan to invite and follow through by checking invitation responses, you will be able to plan easily not only for reception food and beverages but also for seating both in the church and at the reception.

If your wedding is to be at home or in an outdoor setting, you'll also know how many chairs you must borrow or rent and how much parking you should allow.

Keep in mind that many people fail to respond, and understand that you or someone in the wedding party may have to follow up on the guest list a week or so before the wedding by calling those who have not let you know if they will be in attendance.

The job of following up is generally left to the mother of the bride, but this is also a good place to press your maid of honor into service.

If you are planning a large wedding, you may want to prepare a brief "script" for whoever will be doing the telephoning, in order not to get involved in lengthy conversations that make the task too time consuming.

Have the caller say something like this:

"Hello, this is Barbara Jones, Nancy Renno's maid of honor. I'm helping Nan with her final count for the wedding reception. She wants to be prepared for everyone that's planning to attend, and I don't find your name checked off on her guest list yet. Will you be with us at the ceremony? The reception? Who else in your party will be there? [Enter the number of guests and then confirm it.] That's two [or whatever number]? Thank you so much. I know Nan will be delighted to hear you're coming [or sorry to hear you won't be able to attend]. I'm sorry to rush off, but we're having a bridal party meeting tonight, and I want to have the list complete for Nan by then. Thanks again for your help."

The entire follow-up process shouldn't take much more than a minute or two per person if you follow this script, and these calls

can make a big difference in terms of cost and time saving in the last critical days before the wedding.

If you don't think you'll have enough space in the list that follows to include all your guests, copy the format and attach additional pages in the section that follows by stapling them to the blanks.

If the bride has specifically requested that no children be in attendance, this is a good time to remind those who have not responded, tactfully, of that fact.

If the caller finds a guest including children in the number to attend, she can say sweetly, "Oh, I know Nan would love to see little Buster, but she and Don feel a wedding is a very adult occasion. They'd like to have an all-adults day. They are sure you'll understand. It's going to be a lovely ceremony, very meaningful to everyone invited. I'm so glad you'll be there."

If the guest doesn't get the hint, refer her to the bride's mother, and then warn "Mom" that she'll have to restrict the guest list with her best diplomacy.

Once you have a final count of those planning to attend, check that number with your accommodations, parking, catering (or food planning), beverage supply, chair and table service orders, and so on.

You'll find the time spent planning and tracking your guest list will pay off in so many ways. But most of all, a well-kept list will reward you with a well kept budget by allowing you to purchase exactly what you need and not be left with costly extras you can never use again.

Guest List

GUEST'S NAME	ATTENDING	WEDDING	RECEPTION	NEITHER

guest list

Guest List (continued)

GUEST'S NAME	ATTENDING	WEDDING	RECEPTION	NEITHER

5
invitations
or innovations

Once you have set the date and selected a theme and a site for your wedding, invitations must be prepared.

This is an area where costs are extremely hard to cut if you want the formal (or so-called socially proper) engraved or embossed invitations.

Engraved invitations are expensive, running about $50 per hundred, and embossed versions are only a little less at $35 per hundred. The worst of it is, the costs are fixed by printers and stationers who realize that there is little you can do to avoid their services.

There are ways to insure keeping the costs to a minimum, however. First, though your stationer will show you volumes of embossed, gilded, die-cut, and special-fold formats for your invitations, turn a deaf ear to his or her words about these innovations. If you are going to spend money for formal invitations, select the one that is both the least expensive and in the best taste—a single white card or folder.

Using this format, you will still have a choice of a variety of paper weights and shades (pure white to ecru) and edge design from smooth cut to deckled, or perhaps with a raised border. The paper should be a medium weight and of a matte finish, and for formal invitations should always be either white or off-white. Double enve-

lopes are a must and are included in the prices quoted by most reputable firms.

Forget the Enclosures

Next, keep your printing costs down by refusing to add enclosures. Reception cards have come to be considered a must, particularly by stationers and printers who delight in the added revenue this custom brings into their coffers with each wedding order. If your reception is to be held at the same location as the ceremony (and for convenience and keeping costs down this is the best idea anyway) it is possible to have the printer add the phrase "Reception Following" as a footnote to the invitation for about $2 more per hundred. Reception cards to be enclosed separately could run as much as $10 more.

Most stationers and printers will balk at this idea, however, saying that "it is in poor taste" or "simply is not done nowadays." The truth of the matter is that the reason it is not done is that it cuts the printer's profit margin substantially, for printers make a higher percentage on the extras they sell.

If you suggest that a printer might lose your order if he or she refuses the footnote idea, you will find that this entrepreneur will accommodate you rather than risk your taking your business elsewhere. By the week after the wedding no one but you (and perhaps the disgruntled printer) will remember whether you had reception cards enclosed with your invitation or not.

If the cost of formal invitations will put a large dent in your tiny budget, but you still feel they are important, there is a way to have them made at little or (if you are sweet and patient enough) possibly no cost.

Try Student Labor

Check with the graphic arts department of your local high school or college. Or with the nearest trade school that offers graphics as a major. Telephone the instructor and ask for his or her help. If you allow enough time in advance, a teacher may be able to find an outstanding student willing to take on your invitations as a class project for either a little extra cash or extra class credit.

If you do use formal invitations, there are some important things to remember:

1. Formal invitations should be in the mail at least three weeks before the wedding.
2. You will need time before that to address them by hand.
3. All agreements as to deadline and cost, content and format should be in writing.

Beyond this, all you can do is say a prayer and light a candle or cross your fingers that the student you've drawn is a potential pro. Still, even the pros make mistakes occasionally.

A blushing bride I recall had to hold up her ceremony almost an hour waiting for honored guests to arrive, and when the ceremony finally began, the church hall was still half empty. It wasn't until a disgruntled guest pointed out an error in the invitation as he passed through the reception line that the poor girl realized her beautiful invitations—ordered by phone—had listed the church address as being Fir Street rather than Third Street. "Always put it in writing."

Formal Wording

The basic form for wedding invitation content hasn't changed in a century or more. Follow it in formal and informal invitations, and you will be certain that your guests receive all the information they need about your coming nuptials.

The formal invitation is always issued by the bride's parents or by her nearest relative if she is an orphan. The form is as follows:

> *Mr. and Mrs. William Reed*
> *request the honor of your presence*
> *at the marriage of their daughter*
> *Nancy Ann*
> *to*
> *Mr. Donald Curran Renno*
> *on Saturday the sixth of June*
> *at eight o'clock in the evening*
> *St. Thomas Church*
> *117 Park Avenue*
> *New York*
> *Reception Following*

Modifications of this form are made when the bride's parents have been divorced, when they have remarried, if she has been married before, or to reflect other family situations. Your stationer will help you in handling such matters with the utmost taste. Don't be afraid to ask for help; it is part of what you're paying for.

If your wedding will be one of the more informal kinds gaining popularity today, you may not desire the formal invitations that were a status symbol when your parents were married. In this fast-moving era, when doing your own thing is the way to go, you have a right to say no to mom and dad and try something really different for your wedding invitations if you wish.

Photo Process Peels Prices

In your favor is the low-cost photo offset printing process that can give you service while you wait and allows you to compose your entire invitation yourself, using artwork, lettering of any style imaginable, and formats, unheard of in bridal invitation books. Best of all, you get all this freedom for only about $3 per hundred on standard size and weight paper.

In this process you design and lay out your invitation or other piece of printing using a paste-up system. You can use lettering or artwork cut from magazines. You can do your own lettering or artwork using the popular felt-tip pens of varying widths, or you can purchase "art type" rub-on letters or numbers, scrolls, or other fancy work. These are available at art-supply stores for about $1.75 per page, and each page contains several alphabets with multiple vowels, letters, punctuation, and the like. They come in a variety of type faces from block letters to fancy script and Old English. They are fun to use and so simple, too, that even a beginner can achieve professional results with just a little experimentation. Full instructions are included.

Suppose you have selected a Renaissance theme for your wedding and will be stressing a Romeo and Juliet look. Why not try invitations in the form of scrolls using Old English lettering and phrasing of the period, such as:

"Hear ye! Hear ye! Be it known that Mr. and Mrs. William Reed request the honor of your attendance at the nuptials of their daughter

Nancy Ann Reed
and
Donald Curran Renno

on Saturday, the sixth of June, a fortnight hence at eight o'clock in the evening at St. Thomas Church, 117 Park Avenue, New York City.

And be it further known that whereas the joining of these two in holy wedlock is a joyous occasion for one and all, you are hereby invited to attend a reception honoring the couple, immediately following the ceremony, in the church hall.

You could have your parents sign it with a flourish and place a gold seal and a bit of ribbon at the bottom to make it look official. Such scrolls can be mailed in cardboard tubes (no double envelopes!) and are enticing invitations that do much to preview the unique quality you want your wedding to have.

Self-Mailing

For a more modern touch—let's say, an outdoor wedding with a gypsy motif—you might try a script that simulates handwriting (or if yours is up to snuff, use a felt pen) and put together a self-mailing invitation that can be sealed with sealing wax and a zodiac stamp (available at most stationery stores).

To do this, fold a standard $8^{1}/_{2} \times 11$ sheet of paper as you would to insert it into a long envelope, roughly in thirds but with the top flap about an inch-and-a-half from the bottom fold (that's where you put the sealing wax).

Now open the sheet and with the $8^{1}/_{2}$-inch portion at the top as it usually is, put your lettering only in the portion bounded by the two folds—that is, in the middle.

Say something like:

> *In the still of the old oak glen at Canyon Avenue and Woodland Road, Mr. and Mrs. William Reed will give the hand of their daughter Nancy Ann to Donald Curran Renno, at seven in the evening, October the ninth, nineteen hundred and seventy-three.*
>
> *You are invited to celebrate this happy occasion with the families by attending the saying of the vows and the festivities following.*

Such an invitation could feature clipped artwork, such as a tall oak tree, falling leaves, or perhaps just two daisies with stems entwined in a lower corner.

To mail, fold and seal as stated, then with the seal down, address the reverse side as you would an envelope, placing postage in the upper right-hand corner.

A larger self-mailing invitation can be made by folding the pa-

GYPSY MOTIF
Sealed with
Sealing wax &
zodiac sign

per exactly in half and using a gold seal folded over the resulting free edges to hold it together in the mail. In this format use only the bottom half of the paper for your message. Tape or staples are a no! no!

A similarly easy invitation with a "studio card" look is achieved by folding a standard piece of paper lengthwise. This can be used either with the printing on the inside from top to bottom, or side to side, depending on whether you want a tall or a wide look.

Let your imagination run free. Be creative. Make samples of several kinds and take your time until you have just the right look for the mood you are trying to create. Remember, by using this speedy-print process you won't have to wait weeks for your invitations to arrive, so you have time to spare.

Handwritten Notes

If your wedding will be quite small, with only members of the family and a few close friends present, you might not want printed invi-

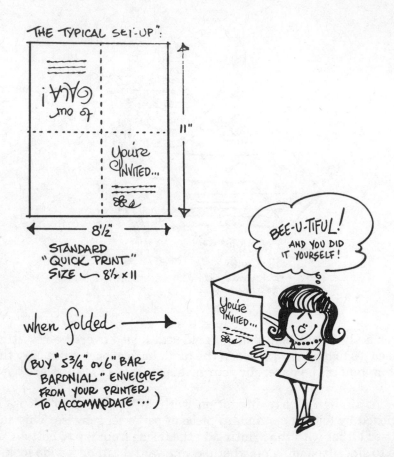

tations at all. You might choose instead to handwrite individual notes to guests asking each to share your special moment with you.

Such notes should be on small white notepaper of a good quality—parchment is nice with one of the narrow-tipped felt pens if your handwriting is good. If not, you might ask grandma or a favorite aunt to handwrite your invitations in her best penmanship for you.

And if you like the handwritten look but need too many to do them individually, again the photo offset process can duplicate your script for pennies each.

A sample note of this kind might say:

Please Share Our Happiness . . .
Don and I will be married Saturday, October 6, in a quiet cere-
mony at my parents' home, 16552 Wanderer Lane, Westchester,
at 8 p.m. We would be honored if you would share our big mo-
ment with us.

Your friend,
Patty

"CUT & PASTE" HEADINGS . . .

A WEDDING!
YOUR OWN
COPY
HERE . . . .

A HAPPY HAPPENING!
A WEDDING!
PLEASE JOIN US . . .
AN INVITATION . . .

In this case it is all right for you to extend the invitation, yourself, to your intimate friends, allowing your mother to invite her personal friends by note in a similar manner, if they are to be included.

Ready-Mades

There are various preprinted multipurpose invitations available that are suitable for either very small informal weddings or anniversaries. These are put out by greeting card companies and usually feature silver bells, or an embossed ring or bell motif on the cover with spaces inside to fill in the date, time, and place of the event.

While certainly not the "socially proper" form for inviting guests to an ultra formal wedding, they may be acceptable for your purposes and are definitely worth considering.

You will find them at most stationery stores of any size, and they have the obvious advantage of being ready made and requiring the minimum of preparation to get them in the mail. So if time is of the essence, these may be for you.

A word of caution here, however. Ready-made invitations of this kind are not as inexpensive as you might think. So if you plan to invite more than 25 guests, you will have far nicer invitations at less cost by using the offset method and it's almost as fast.

If you are eager for something really spectacular that will look as if it cost a mint but won't put a significant dent in your budget, consider combining ready-made "blanks" with a customized printing that you design yourself.

These blanks are beautiful full color lithographs of wedding scenes, such as hands atop a bridal bouquet; a man and woman silhouetted against a sunset, kissing; a single rose held in the hand of a bride; a pair of gold bands sitting before a prayer book surrounded by flowers; and so on.

They are published by several major lithographers throughout the United States and distributed through religious-supply stores. Because they are printed by the millions, the cost is a fraction of what you could afford to do yourself. And, as they are printed only on one side and designed to be folded in half (a standard $8^1/2 \times 11$

sheet, which folds to 8 $^1/_2$ × 5$^1/_2$) like a large greeting card, they are perfect for personalization on the unprinted inside.

If you are a regular churchgoer, you may have seen these, as they are bridal versions of the programs some churches hand out when people enter on Sunday morning, the colorful leaflets that contain the service for the day.

Among the publishers who distribute these are: CPH Litho, Christian Art, Augeburg Publishing House, The Hermitage Art Co., and Panoramic Focus Bulletins.

Ask your minister where he or she purchases the weekly church bulletin blanks, or check the Yellow Pages for religious supply stores.

You will find a treasury of styles, photos, and imprinted verses to choose from, including those with Bible verses and those without, and some with sayings such as "Two Shall Become One" or "Today Our Love Is Made Perfect."

One of my favorites is a table-top still life of a page of sheet music featuring "The Wedding Prayer," surrounded by a pink and white nosegay, ribbons, lace, and lighted candelabra. Another, perfect for an outdoor ceremony, simply features a golden butterfly perched upon a flower and featuring the saying "We Too Might Walk In The Newness of Life."

So, before you shell out a large share of your budget for exotic invitations that are highly touted by printers, take a look at these which you can individualize yourself. You might even find the perfect theme for your wedding, among them.

In addition to invitations, many brides-to-be have other printing they want done. If you plan to order imprinted napkins for your reception, plastic tableware, plates, matches, remembrance poems, thank-you notes or other items that will constitute a large printing order, don't be afraid to ask for a discount.

The worst that can happen is that you will be turned down, but many printing houses offer bridal "packages" at a reduced rate or will throw in a small item, such as match covers, if your order is large enough. Few will advise you of this practice unless you press them on it, however. So press on!

6
have a working wedding party

One of the biggest assets a bride on a budget can have is a working wedding party.

Thoroughly involving bridesmaids, ushers, and other members of the wedding party in preparations for your big day can add measurably to the event and subtract substantially from the total costs if you select your "crew" carefully.

The tendency is to "think small" in selecting the wedding party of a bride on a budget, but this is one instance when those with the Volkswagen philosophy are way off base. Having a dozen willing workers is well worth the expense of extra flowers and the like when you consider the luxury effect a large wedding party creates and the time and money that can be saved by turning the members of the party loose on the myriad little tasks that must be done in the course of wedding preparations.

Who your attendants will be, and how many you will include in your wedding party, should be weighed carefully before the final selections are made. You may long for a childhood chum from a distant town to be your maid of honor. But before you dash off an invitation to her, consider the fact that she'll probably be in town only a day or two before the ceremony, and not only will be unable to help you out when you need help most but may create added work for you and added costs (for example, lodging, meals, special rehearsal times) when you can least afford them.

Your maid of honor should be your "good right-hand man." She should be the captain of your team, someone you can trust to handle special assignments with care and to follow through without fail on long-range plans.

The best man, likewise, should be selected with care. The people you put in these positions of responsibility should be the kind of unshakable souls who can be expected to come through with flying colors when all around them are failing fast—including you!

Select with Care

In choosing members of your wedding party, you will draw from three basic resource or talent pools: friends, family, and future in-laws. Ideally, the party should include a mixture of all three. How many is strictly up to you and may be determined on the basis of a

number of factors. A rule of thumb, here, is one bridesmaid or usher, in addition to the maid of honor and best man, for each fifty invited guests.

Almost as soon as the engagement ring is on your finger, you will begin mentally screening for these important jobs. Give your head equal time with your heart in making the final decisions, however, remembering that willing hands are far more important than pretty faces in making your wedding sparkle.

List relatives, friends, and members of your future husband's family that you would consider for spots in your wedding, then sit down with your fiancé (some evening when you're saving money for your honeymoon by not going to a movie) and talk objectively about each one.

Make notes regarding the relative time each would have to devote to duties before the wedding, his or her proximity to the hub of prenuptial activity, talents or skills she or he might have to offer, and the reliability quotient of each of your potential participants. You will undoubtedly be surprised at the divergent skills represented, and you may be encouraged to expand your wedding party to include some extra members on the basis of such a list. You may, on the other hand, rule out some emotional choices or reduce their roles when you look frankly at how little they would or could contribute.

Try This Test

All this may sound cold and callous. But when you consider that being chosen out of all the people in the world to be a part of your day of days is really quite an honor, you should feel quite justified in applying the following test to potential candidates for the positions you have to fill:

1. Will the attendant be available to carry out prenuptial duties? Does she live nearby, have a car, and so on?
2. Will she be willing and able to follow through on specific requests, such as addressing envelopes, cooking, or baking?

ENTHUSIASM · CREATIVITY ~ WARMTH & SENTIMENTALITY

3. Will she have special skills or talents to contribute, such as musical talent, cake decorating, sewing?
4. Will she give freely of her time and talents?

If the answer to all these questions is an unqualified yes, you have a real jewel, a definite candidate for maid of honor. But before you put someone in this post, add up answers to these questions as well:

1. Does she have a definite quality of leadership?
2. Can you depend on her without reservation?

If so, she's the one. If not, try again. For above all else, your honor attendant and best man both must be the type who can muster the crew and, second only to you, inspire them with the joy and fun of the duties to be done.

What are the duties to be done? That's for you to decide. There can be as many or as few as your budget demands, as important as baking the cake or as trivial as tying the tin cans on the car, but they should be spelled out and assigned early in the game.

Don't be afraid to holler "help"—and often—if you have selected a group that will really constitute a working wedding party.

Begin by letting members in on your needs at the time you invite them. Let them know that one of the reasons you have selected them to be a part of your special day is because they are very special to you in some way. Let them know you recognize their specific skills and talents and ask their advice on matters in which they have expertise. You will probably find that, before you can work up courage to ask them to take over needed assignments, they will be asking what they can do to help. If you have put each to the test mentioned here, you will have an answer ready.

Put the Crew to Work

If attendant A is an evening school student with days free and access to a car, put her to work doing some comparative shopping for flowers, decorations, bakeries, etc., during the day. Having someone to do preliminary legwork for you can be a godsend.

Perhaps attendant B is occupied by work or school during the day but has evenings free. Have her address wedding invitations, scan recipe books for reception menu ideas, or make and freeze hors d'oeuvres.

Suppose there is a musician or singer in the group. Put her to work selecting a variety of her best songs, then ask her to perform at the wedding or receptioin.

If you are lucky enough to have a truly handy individual in your wedding party—one skilled with a needle and thread or crochet hook—put her to work whipping up headpieces for the other attendants (to your specifications, of course), or assisting them in making their gowns.

An artist in the wedding party can be put to work making a unique "Just Married" sign for your car or decorating posters to adorn the reception hall.

Put your matron of honor in charge of supervising these tasks and give her a master list of who has agreed to do what. Her job can be to make sure assignments are accomplished by the appointed deadlines. That is a full-time job, at least!

She might also arrange for a work party or two when all members of the wedding party would gather to work together on a major task, such as preparing food, production-line style, for the reception; making church and reception decorations; sewing lace appliqués on your gown; or other time-consuming activities.

A bit of cake and punch can turn such work sessions into modern versions of the "quilting bee" of grandma's day, when everyone pitched in to help and had a ball doing it.

Such work parties don't have to be limited to members of the formal wedding party. Grandmothers, aunts, and cousins, who are often overlooked during the hectic days prior to the wedding, are generally delighted to be included in the advance preparations this way.

Don't forget to invite your future mother-in-law, too, for such a gathering is a great way for her to get to know your family and close friends better. It's a great way, too, for her to see you in your best light, with friends gathered around to show their fondness for you by giving of their time and talents. She may even begin to think you might be good enough for her "faultless, fair-haired boy."

Even the youngest members of the wedding party should be given advance tasks to do. Your altar boys or ring bearers can be put in charge of assembling an assortment of tin cans and old shoes for your honeymoon car. The flower girl or junior bridesmaid can cut crepe-paper streamers to festoon the reception hall. Catch on? The point is that everyone will be happier and have less to do if nobody is left out.

Help Wanted: Male

Ushers and the best man can help in a hundred ways. They can take over such tasks as polishing the cars for your wedding motorcade, arranging musical entertainment for the reception, serving as bartenders or wine stewards at the reception, providing transportation for food and decorations to the wedding or reception site, offering a shuttle service to guests where parking is a problem, or acting as pickup and delivery men for the myriad items you may have to rent or borrow for the wedding and postnuptial party.

In order to prevent chaos, make certain you have a copy of the master duty roster and post it where you can refer to it regularly—by the phone is a good place—checking off items as they are done. Check with your attendants regularly and have a summit conference with your maid of honor at least once a week until all major items on the schedule are complete.

Set the Pace

List your own duties on the roster and be a shining example to your troops by plunging in with religious fervor until they are all done well in advance of deadlines. You'll feel better about everything, and more relaxed, if you have at least a week before the wedding to contemplate the joy of it all and concentrate on making yourself beautiful for your big day.

After your master list is complete, go over it carefully, with an eye to seeing to it that no one has taken on more than she can possibly do, just because she is a sweetheart! Make certain, too, that everyone on the list has at least one item to take care of that can be pointed to with pride at the wedding or reception as her own special contribution to the gala event.

In selecting your wedding party from the pool of family, future family, and friends available, you may find people you will want to include in capacities other than those of bridesmaids, ushers, and honor attendants.

Children Add Charm but ...

There are a number of other roles important people in your life can play—roles that will add uniquely to your wedding.

A flower girl and ring bearer are always fun additions to the entourage, for the duties performed by such small fry always add a note of intrigue to the ceremony by keeping guests guessing just what they might do.

One ring bearer who sneezed loudly during the prayer portion of an elaborate wedding ceremony I attended turned politely to the pastor and said with a smile, "You'd better start over, Father, and bless me, too!" It was a priceless moment no one could have foreseen and one that was talked of time and time again for years. Another little boy, whose angelic performance at the wedding rehearsal of his sister was highly praised, turned up at the wedding with a shiner of gigantic proportions, adding a distinct note of whimsy to the wedding and a priceless touch to the formal photos as well.

Youngsters asked to perform as flower girls and ring bearers should not be less than four years of age if you want whimsy and not chaos, however. And generally they should be no older than ten, for after that they are closer in size to the adult attendants and can be pressed into service in the more mature roles of junior ushers or junior bridesmaids.

Brothers and sisters of the bride and bridegroom (particularly the younger siblings) should be included in the ceremony somehow, if at all possible.

They can serve as acolytes (altar boys or girls) to light candles in the church or assist the minister, as pages following along behind the bride and her father, carrying her train or cathedral-length veil; as guest book attendants; or official greeters, distributing remembrance poems and ushering guests into the church where they will be shown to their seats by the ushers; or as mini–door attendants.

If there is simply no duty you can find for the younger members of the family at the church or wedding site, press them into service at the reception, allowing them to pass refreshments, serve punch, or distribute rice bags for the shower of rice that generally takes place these days after the reception rather than as the couple leaves the church. (Most churches frown on the mess it leaves on their grounds.)

Putting the younger members of the family to work in such ways has an added bonus—busy children are less apt to find mischief or to wind up cranky and unpleasant after the initial excitement of the ceremony wears off.

Be Appreciative

Finally, no matter what the duty or how small the wedding party member who performs it, let him or her know you truly appreciate the service. Be enthusiastic about even the most menial jobs. Be lavish with your praise. A whispered "thanks" with a kiss in the reception line can make it all worthwhile to those who have given of their time. But it doesn't hurt to follow it up with a thank-you note in writing. A small gift to each member of the wedding party, with a little something special for those who have really done a great job, will let them know you're the angel they were certain you were before all the work began.

A word of caution, here, however. Don't let any grass grow under your feet in getting your thank-you notes out, and no matter how tired or cranky you may feel, be sweet to those who are trying to help you—you'll never regret it.

7

your wedding expense register

As you make the final decision on each of the desired items for your wedding, enter the name of the vendor or lender, the address, telephone number, the date you must make final payment or return the rented item, and the final cost.

On rented items, enter the amount of deposit required as well, and if it is a refundable deposit, note that also. Rented items should also be entered with borrowed items in the Return Register, which follows the Wedding Expense Register in this chapter. These items should be dated as returned and the amount of refund entered if the item is rented, or the date that the thank-you note is sent if it is a borrowed item.

Special care should be taken with rented or borrowed items. One broken "treasure" that must be replaced to a vendor or lender can up the cost of your wedding substantially. So, if you borrow a lead-crystal punch bowl that had been in Aunt Sophie's family for a century, for heaven's sake, take tender loving care of it. No amount of repayment can compensate for the loss or destruction of a family heirloom!

Make sure that all rented or borrowed items are returned clean and polished (particularly silver) and in perfect working condition.

And, if friends or relatives are kind enough to volunteer needed items or services, make certain you return them promptly and with a special note of thanks. The registers that follow are designed to help you accomplish all of this with ease.

When considering the division of wedding expenses, the old rule was that the bride's family bore the lion's share of wedding costs, with the groom's family paying only for flowers and liquor.

Today, almost anything goes. Many couples choose to pay for their own weddings completely, to avoid a financial burden on their parents and to maintain control of the plans.

In other families, the groom's parents may be better able to afford wedding costs than the bride's and volunteer to pick up the entire tab. Frequently, the two families split the cost. Nothing is taboo anymore.

Often generous grandparents or other relatives offer to pay a portion of the expense, and this is not only acceptable, it is divine!

And frequently, brides on a budget may ask their attendants to pay for their own gowns (or to make them), shoes, and headpieces. If this is done, however, the bride or her family should supply the attendants with all desired accessories, necklaces, flowers, and the like.

The groom, best man, and ushers generally pay for their own tuxedo rental. And often the best man will provide the limousine rental for the wedding, but he should not be asked to do so if he doesn't volunteer. He may choose to honor the groom with a bachelor party or some other special gift, and that is up to him.

However the wedding expenses are divided, be certain to acknowledge those who have helped to make your wedding day special. They deserve your gratitude for helping to make your special day affordable, so give it freely.

Wedding Expense Register

ITEM	VENDOR/LENDER	ADDRESS	PHONE	DATE DUE	FINAL COST	$
Wedding Gown						$
Veil and Headpiece						$
Flowers						$
Tux Rental						$
Mother's Gown						$
Bridesmaids' Gowns						$
Limo Rental						$
Minister's Fee						$
Wedding Cake						$
Food						$
Beverages						$
Invitations						$
Postage						$

Wedding Expense Register (continued)

ITEM	VENDOR/LENDER	ADDRESS	PHONE	DATE DUE	FINAL COST
Flower Girl's Dress					$
Attendants' Hats					$
Church Rental					$
Reception Hall					$
Soloist					$
Organist					$
Thank-You Notes					$
Photographer/Photos					$
Albums					$
Rings					$
Attendants' Gifts					$

Band _____ $ _____

License _____ $ _____

Equipment Rental _____ $ _____

_____ $ _____

_____ $ _____

Hired Help _____ $ _____

Gratuities _____ $ _____

Honeymoon Hotel _____ $ _____

Transportation _____ $ _____

Travel Wardrobe _____ $ _____

Beauty Aids _____ $ _____

Alterations _____ $ _____

Miscellaneous _____ $ _____

GRAND TOTAL $ _____

Wedding Expense Register (continued)

TO BE DIVIDED AMONG

BRIDE'S PARENTS, Items: _____ $_____

GROOM'S PARENTS, Items: _____ $_____

BRIDE, Items: _____ $_____

GROOM, Items: _____ $_____

Bride's Grandparents, Item: _____ $_____

Grooms' Grandparents, Item: _____ $_____

Attendants, Items: _____ $_____

Others Who Want to Help, Item: _____ $_____

Return Register for Borrowed or Rented Items

ITEM	DATE BORROWED	DATE RETURNED	THANK-YOU DATE OR DEPOSIT RETURNED

In order to keep wedding costs within your bridal budget, use the following worksheets to compare prices, keep track of costs, and enter alternatives. Use the completed sample below as a guide.

As you make final purchases, rentals, or arrangements for borrowing needed items, cross them off the work sheets and enter them in the Wedding Expense Register, along with the actual costs, rental fees, or name and address of the lender.

Then, when your wedding is complete, you'll have a written record of your expenses and of those items that must be returned to rental agents or lenders. And you'll have a record of your savings as well!

Sample Bridal Budget Worksheet

ITEM	COST	COMPARISON BY SHOP	ALTERNATIVES	COST
WEDDING GOWN	1. $850.00	Shop Name Bride's Way	1. Copy it!	1. $120.00
	2. $595.00	Shop Name Macy's	2. Rent it!	2. $ 85.00
	3. $125.00	Shop Name Recycled Duds	3. Wear Mom's	3. $ —0—
Final Decision: Wear Mom's wedding gown and have it altered				$ 35.00
VEIL AND HEADPIECE	1. $175.00	Shop Name Bridetique	1. Buy hat only	1. $ 75.00
	2. $129.95	Shop Name Gimbles	2. Make veil	2. $ 20.00
	3. $ 15.00	Shop Name Goodwill	3. Buy it!	3. $ 15.00
Final Decision: Purchase from Goodwill thrift shop and freshen				$ 25.00
FLOWERS	1. $1,250	Florist Artistic Flora	1. Cut down	1. $?
	2. $ 325.00	Florist Flowers By Ann	2. Do own	2. $150.00
	3. $ 85.00	Florist Ted's Produce	3. Buy supplies	3. $ 25.00
Final Decision: Buy flowers and supplies and do own arrangements				$110.00

Bridal Budget Worksheets

ITEM	COST COMPARISON BY SHOP	ALTERNATIVES	COST
WEDDING GOWN	1. $ _____ Shop Name _____	1. _____	1. $ _____
	2. $ _____ Shop Name _____	2. _____	2. $ _____
	3. $ _____ Shop Name _____	3. _____	3. $ _____
Final Decision:			$ _____
VEIL AND HEADPIECE	1. $ _____ Shop Name _____	1. _____	1. $ _____
	2. $ _____ Shop Name _____	2. _____	2. $ _____
	3. $ _____ Shop Name _____	3. _____	3. $ _____
Final Decision:			$ _____
FLOWERS	1. $ _____ Shop Name _____	1. _____	1. $ _____
	2. $ _____ Shop Name _____	2. _____	2. $ _____
	3. $ _____ Shop Name _____	3. _____	3. $ _____
Final Decision:			$ _____
TUX RENTAL	1. $ _____ Shop Name _____	1. _____	1. $ _____
	2. $ _____ Shop Name _____	2. _____	2. $ _____
	3. $ _____ Shop Name _____	3. _____	3. $ _____
Final Decision: _____			$ _____

MOTHER'S GOWN

1. $ _____   Shop Name _____   1. $ _____
2. $ _____   Shop Name _____   2. $ _____
3. $ _____   Shop Name _____   3. $ _____

Final Decision: _____ $ _____

BRIDESMAIDS' GOWNS

1. $ _____   Shop Name _____   1. $ _____
2. $ _____   Shop Name _____   2. $ _____
3. $ _____   Shop Name _____   3. $ _____

Final Decision: _____ $ _____

LIMO RENTAL

1. $ _____   Shop Name _____   1. $ _____
2. $ _____   Shop Name _____   2. $ _____
3. $ _____   Shop Name _____   3. $ _____

Final Decision: _____ $ _____

MINISTER'S FEE

1. $ _____   Shop Name _____   1. $ _____
2. $ _____   Shop Name _____   2. $ _____
3. $ _____   Shop Name _____   3. $ _____

Final Decision: _____ $ _____

Bridal Budget Worksheets (continued)

ITEM	COST COMPARISON BY SHOP		ALTERNATIVES	COST
WEDDING CAKE	1. $ _____ Shop Name _____		1. _____	1. $ _____
	2. $ _____ Shop Name _____		2. _____	2. $ _____
	3. $ _____ Shop Name _____		3. _____	3. $ _____
Final Decision:				$ _____
RECEPTION FOOD (or catering)	1. $ _____ Shop Name _____		1. _____	1. $ _____
	2. $ _____ Shop Name _____		2. _____	2. $ _____
	3. $ _____ Shop Name _____		3. _____	3. $ _____
Final Decision:				$ _____
LIQUOR AND OTHER BEVERAGES	1. $ _____ Shop Name _____		1. _____	1. $ _____
	2. $ _____ Shop Name _____		2. _____	2. $ _____
	3. $ _____ Shop Name _____		3. _____	3. $ _____
Final Decision:				$ _____
INVITATIONS AND POSTAGE	1. $ _____ Shop Name _____		1. _____	1. $ _____
	2. $ _____ Shop Name _____		2. _____	2. $ _____
	3. $ _____ Shop Name _____		3. _____	3. $ _____
Final Decision:				$ _____

FLOWER GIRL'S DRESS

1. $ _____   Shop Name _____   1. _____

2. $ _____   Shop Name _____   2. _____

3. $ _____   Shop Name _____   3. _____

Final Decision: _____ $ _____

ATTENDANTS' HEADPIECES

1. $ _____   Shop Name _____   1. _____

2. $ _____   Shop Name _____   2. _____

3. $ _____   Shop Name _____   3. _____

Final Decision: _____ $ _____

CHURCH RENTAL

1. $ _____   Shop Name _____   1. _____

2. $ _____   Shop Name _____   2. _____

3. $ _____   Shop Name _____   3. _____

Final Decision: _____ $ _____

RECEPTION SITE RENTAL FEES

1. $ _____   Shop Name _____   1. _____

2. $ _____   Shop Name _____   2. _____

3. $ _____   Shop Name _____   3. _____

Final Decision: _____ $ _____

Bridal Budget Worksheets (continued)

ITEM	COST COMPARISON BY SHOP	ALTERNATIVES	COST
SOLOIST	1. $ _____ Shop Name _____	1. _____	1. $ _____
	2. $ _____ Shop Name _____	2. _____	2. $ _____
	3. $ _____ Shop Name _____	3. _____	3. $ _____
Final Decision:			$ _____
ORGANIST	1. $ _____ Shop Name _____	1. _____	1. $ _____
	2. $ _____ Shop Name _____	2. _____	2. $ _____
	3. $ _____ Shop Name _____	3. _____	3. $ _____
Final Decision:			$ _____
THANK-YOU NOTES	1. $ _____ Shop Name _____	1. _____	1. $ _____
	2. $ _____ Shop Name _____	2. _____	2. $ _____
	3. $ _____ Shop Name _____	3. _____	3. $ _____
Final Decision:			$ _____
PHOTOGRAPHER	1. $ _____ Shop Name _____	1. _____	1. $ _____
	2. $ _____ Shop Name _____	2. _____	2. $ _____
	3. $ _____ Shop Name _____	3. _____	3. $ _____
Final Decision:			$ _____

PHOTOS

1. $ _____	Shop Name _____	1. _____ $ _____
2. $ _____	Shop Name _____	2. _____ $ _____
3. $ _____	Shop Name _____	3. _____ $ _____
		$ _____

Final Decision: _____

ALBUM

1. $ _____	Shop Name _____	1. _____ $ _____
2. $ _____	Shop Name _____	2. _____ $ _____
3. $ _____	Shop Name _____	3. _____ $ _____
		$ _____

Final Decision: _____

GIFT ALBUMS

1. $ _____	Shop Name _____	1. _____ $ _____
2. $ _____	Shop Name _____	2. _____ $ _____
3. $ _____	Shop Name _____	3. _____ $ _____
		$ _____

Final Decision: _____

WEDDING RINGS

1. $ _____	Shop Name _____	1. _____ $ _____
2. $ _____	Shop Name _____	2. _____ $ _____
3. $ _____	Shop Name _____	3. _____ $ _____
		$ _____

Final Decision: _____

Bridal Budget Worksheets (continued)

ITEM	COST COMPARISON BY SHOP	ALTERNATIVES	COST
ATTENDANTS' GIFTS	1. $ _____ Shop Name _____	1. _____	1. $ _____
	2. $ _____ Shop Name _____	2. _____	2. $ _____
	3. $ _____ Shop Name _____	3. _____	3. $ _____
Final Decision: _____			$ _____
BAND FOR RECEPTION	1. $ _____ Shop Name _____	1. _____	1. $ _____
	2. $ _____ Shop Name _____	2. _____	2. $ _____
	3. $ _____ Shop Name _____	3. _____	3. $ _____
Final Decision: _____			$ _____
MARRIAGE LICENSE	1. $ _____ Shop Name _____	1. _____	1. $ _____
	2. $ _____ Shop Name _____	2. _____	2. $ _____
	3. $ _____ Shop Name _____	3. _____	3. $ _____
Final Decision: _____			$ _____
EQUIPMENT RENTAL (tables and chairs, linens and so on)	1. $ _____ Shop Name _____	1. _____	1. $ _____
	2. $ _____ Shop Name _____	2. _____	2. $ _____
	3. $ _____ Shop Name _____	3. _____	3. $ _____
Final Decision: _____			$ _____

HIRED HELP
(bartender, waiters, master of ceremonies)

1. $	Shop Name	1.	1. $
2. $	Shop Name	2.	2. $
3. $	Shop Name	3.	3. $

Final Decision: _____ $ _____

GRATUITIES

1. $	Shop Name	1.	1. $
2. $	Shop Name	2.	2. $
3. $	Shop Name	3.	3. $

Final Decision: _____ $ _____

HONEYMOON HOTEL

1. $	Shop Name	1.	1. $
2. $	Shop Name	2.	2. $
3. $	Shop Name	3.	3. $

Final Decision: _____ $ _____

TRANSPORTATION
(air fare, car rentals, and so on)

1. $	Shop Name	1.	1. $
2. $	Shop Name	2.	2. $
3. $	Shop Name	3.	3. $

Final Decision: _____ $ _____

Bridal Budget Worksheets (continued)

ITEM	COST COMPARISON BY SHOP		ALTERNATIVES	COST
TRAVEL WARDROBE	1. $ _____	Shop Name _____	1. _____	1. $ _____
	2. $ _____	Shop Name _____	2. _____	2. $ _____
	3. $ _____	Shop Name _____	3. _____	3. $ _____
Final Decision:				$ _____
BEAUTY AIDS (hair styling, manicure, and so on)	1. $ _____	Shop Name _____	1. _____	1. $ _____
	2. $ _____	Shop Name _____	2. _____	2. $ _____
	3. $ _____	Shop Name _____	3. _____	3. $ _____
Final Decision:				$ _____
ALTERATIONS (shoe dyeing, hemming, fitting, and so on)	1. $ _____	Shop Name _____	1. _____	1. $ _____
	2. $ _____	Shop Name _____	2. _____	2. $ _____
	3. $ _____	Shop Name _____	3. _____	3. $ _____
Final Decision:				$ _____
MISCELLANEOUS	1. $ _____	Shop Name _____	1. _____	1. $ _____
	2. $ _____	Shop Name _____	2. _____	2. $ _____
	3. $ _____	Shop Name _____	3. _____	3. $ _____
Final Decision:				$ _____

MISCELLANEOUS   1. $ _____   Shop Name _____   1. $ _____

   2. $ _____   Shop Name _____   2. $ _____

   3. $ _____   Shop Name _____   3. $ _____

         $ _____

Final Decision: _____

MISCELLANEOUS   1. $ _____   Shop Name _____   1. $ _____

   2. $ _____   Shop Name _____   2. $ _____

   3. $ _____   Shop Name _____   3. $ _____

         $ _____

Final Decision: _____

MISCELLANEOUS   1. $ _____   Shop Name _____   1. $ _____

   2. $ _____   Shop Name _____   2. $ _____

   3. $ _____   Shop Name _____   3. $ _____

         $ _____

Final Decision: _____

MISCELLANEOUS   1. $ _____   Shop Name _____   1. $ _____

   2. $ _____   Shop Name _____   2. $ _____

   3. $ _____   Shop Name _____   3. $ _____

         $ _____

Final Decision: _____

Bridal Budget Worksheets (continued)

ITEM	COST COMPARISON BY SHOP	ALTERNATIVES	COST
MISCELLANEOUS	1. $ _____ Shop Name _____	1. _____	1. $ _____
	2. $ _____ Shop Name _____	2. _____	2. $ _____
	3. $ _____ Shop Name _____	3. _____	3. $ _____
Final Decision:			$ _____
MISCELLANEOUS	1. $ _____ Shop Name _____	1. _____	1. $ _____
	2. $ _____ Shop Name _____	2. _____	2. $ _____
	3. $ _____ Shop Name _____	3. _____	3. $ _____
Final Decision:			$ _____

8
great gowns
for pennies apiece

The bridal gown is often the single most expensive item in a wedding budget. It doesn't have to be.

This is an area where there are myriad ways to economize, one where hundreds of dollars can be saved without sacrificing the beauty of the bride in any way.

Some of the most picturesque brides I have known were girls who went to the altar in gowns that didn't cost them a cent. Wearing sentimental "hand-me-down gowns" worn previously by a relative or close friend, these girls saved the entire cost of their bridal costumes while adding a measure of warmth to their weddings that money couldn't buy.

You may not have a fairy godmother to spin you a gown Cinderella-style, but there may be a gown in the family already that could make you look like a princess on your wedding day.

Sew and Save

If the gowns you might borrow aren't suitable, or would have to be altered extensively, consider the course of a frugal but talented bride I recall who bought herself an expensive sewing machine rather than a high-priced wedding dress.

With the machine which "did everything but supply the

groom" she whipped up an original for less than the cost of the machine. Few of her wedding guests knew she had made her wedding gown budget do double duty, and those who did congratulated her on both her beautiful ensemble and her honest practicality.

If you are all thumbs, or simply haven't the time or talent it takes to create your own gown, check with the home economics departments of the community colleges or high schools nearest your home. Often, advanced sewing and design students will take on a wedding gown to earn extra cash or class credit. Such aspiring seamstresses will usually go out of their way to make gowns exactly to your specifications for tiny price tags if you furnish the materials and the patience for frequent fittings and consultations.

Give a Gown a Second Chance

Bridal gowns are seldom worn more than once, but when you consider all the love and care that go into their creation, giving one a second chance seems only fitting.

In addition to the hand-me-down or heirloom gowns that may be borrowed, thrift shops in almost every city have gowns to offer at pennies per dollar of their original cost. At four such shops within a three-mile radius of each other I found five in one day. All were in near perfect condition, and several had matching veils, ring pillows, detachable trains, and other accessories. The most expensive was $50; most were under $25; and I even found one charmer the salesperson called a "fixer upper" for $5. It had tiny holes in the netting in several places on the train, but the clerk offered the advice that one could remove a lace under-panel and clip appliqués from it, which could be used to cover the holes and decorate the rest of the train—and no one would ever be the wiser. The lace and satin in the gown alone were worth well over the asking price.

Purchasing a gown from a thrift shop is even less expensive, in most instances, than renting one. And if you choose wisely you may be selecting an heirloom gown for a future bride in the family.

A college coed whose satin Harlow-style gown was a real knockout confided that she had bought the antique-white creation at a campus rummage sale for $3.

A bit of freshening at a local cleaner plus accessories of the era, including six yards of tulle attached to a crown of wax-dipped orange blossoms for her headdress, brought the total cost to under $50. It was a million-dollar look, however, and she was a platinum blonde bride never to be forgotten.

If you select a gown from another era, remember that you should accessorize it and dress your attendants accordingly. A trip to the local library will provide inspiration. There are many books available with photos and illustrations of women's clothing of other times. You will find, too, that fabrics of days gone by were simpler and less expensive than those usually selected for weddings today. Authenticity, here, is a grand excuse for maximum savings.

"The Hand-Me-Up-Gown"

If you are the eldest of several sisters, the first to be wed of a circle of engaged friends on budgets, or one of several cousins planning marriage in the not-too-distant future, consider the "Hand-Me-Up" gown.

The idea is the same as the hand-me-down, only in reverse. Get together with your sisters, friends, cousins, or other relatives who are planning their weddings (yes, even if they haven't picked out the groom yet), and go shopping for a gown that will be suitable for two or three or more women—then split the cost!

I have a delightful friend with four sisters who did just this, and in doing so has created a genuine heirloom which each hopes her own daughter will wear some day.

Because they were willing to split the cost of the gown, they each were able to wear a dress that none of them could have afforded on their own. Because they planned ahead, they bought the gown in the largest size needed, and had it altered carefully so that it could be let out and taken in as needed to fit each one perfectly on her wedding day. And, so as not to be carbon copies of each other, each bride-to-be selected a different hat and veil of her own. They put the gown on lay-away almost a year before the first wedding, and each paid a payment on alternate months until the gown and five head pieces were paid in full.

To further alter the look of the gown during the various weddings that ensued, one bride chose to wear it without the detachable train, another removed the white sash and replaced it with a mauve velvet sash, the third added a huge hoop petticoat, and the fourth a lace overskirt.

Smart women! And sentimental, too. They each served as bridesmaids for the others and thoroughly enjoyed watching their wedding gown in rerun all the more for having shared in its cost and selection.

This same idea might be extended to include the bridesmaids' gowns if attendants are to be exclusively family members. And if mom and dad are picking up the tab for three or four weddings in a span of four or five years, they'll be certain to be your biggest boosters in this kind of clever endeavour.

So, hand-me-up or hand-me-down, you'll find lots of ways to save on your wedding gown!

Break Tradition and Save

If you are making your own gown or having it made, consider similar savings by turning your back on the imported satins and laces touted by bridal consultants in the "best" stores. Realizing that your gown will probably be worn only once, don't waste money on fabrics that will "wear like iron." What you want is a soft, feminine look, and the inexpensive synthetic blends, light and airy sheers, or frosted organdies can produce that look for a fraction of the cost of more traditional fabrics.

Brides who choose offbeat motifs for their weddings often find built-in excuses to save. An exceptionally beautiful wedding I attended the year Hawaii was admitted to the Union featured costumes of the new state, which was the honeymoon destination of the bride and groom.

The attendants wore gaily colored print gowns of cotton, fitted in front and flowing freely to the floor in back. The bride's gown mimicked the style but was fashioned in white brocade.

The bride and her attendants all wore floral wreaths in their hair and the traditional flower leis around their necks. Adding to the striking effect, each girl carried an additional lei, which she presented to her partner in the wedding party as they met in front of the altar before the ceremony. Only the bride reserved her floral gift until the vows were said, presenting it to her husband when the minister announced the time for the wedding kiss.

The groom and his party took up the island dress-of-the-day, too, donning white slacks and short-sleeved white shirts for the ceremony and wearing bright cummerbunds matching the attire of the bride and her attendants. With their floral leis around their necks, they helped complete a wedding picture none who witnessed it will forget.

The bride's mother confessed later that the exquisite gowns that were admired so much had been bought at a local discount store for less than $10 each and the bride's gown had been copied from their design by a talented aunt at under $15.

What was saved by sticking to the island theme in attire made up enough to splurge on the flowers and on a luau-style reception in the garden where the wedding was performed.

Black Culture Clothing

Black couples in many sections of the country are taking to black culture clothing for interesting and meaningful weddings that are spectacular to behold. Using authentic African designs for robes of both bride and groom and hand-painted fabrics available at import shops, more and more couples are bringing the drama of their African ancestry to the altar with pride.

According to a recent bride who chose this theme for her wedding, "White on white may be all right for some brides but, baby, that's not where it's at in my neighborhood!"

Almost anyone can assemble the clean, simple African robes for a Black Culture ceremony even if they've never sewn a stitch before. There is little fitting to be done, and costumes for both men and women in the wedding party can be put together from scissors to hem in a matter of hours.

A little research will provide a variety of authentic African wedding costumes to select from, and once again a trip to the library is well worth the car fare.

Instant Patterns

If research just isn't your bag, try one of these African styles. Both are almost "instant" patterns and can be adapted for the bridesmaids as well, using a different fabric or color.

1. To create a form-fitting African gown for the bride or female members of her wedding party, purchase four yards of 45-inch material for each gown, cutting a 45-inch square from one end of each four-yard length.

Divide the square diagonally in half (into two equilateral triangles) and narrowly hem each edge, then set them aside.

Hand-hem the unselvaged edges of the remaining fabric (slightly less than three yards) and, using safety pins to anchor it securely, have your mother or a friend drape the fabric tightly around your body from underarms to knees, then loosely to the floor, hiding the pins as she goes.

When she has achieved a look you like, tie one of the triangles at an angle around your hips and the other either over your shoulders (tucking the ends into the bodice of your "instant" gown) or as a headdress.

For quite a different look, try this easy style . . .

2. Using fabric at least 45-inches wide, purchase a length that is double the distance from your shoulder to the floor, plus two inches. If you are of average height (5'4" to 5'6"), this will be slightly more than three yards.

Fold the fabric crossways exactly in half so that the unselvaged edges are together at the bottom and the fold is at the top. Cut a semicircle from the center fold large enough to accommodate your neck, then slash the front of the opening six inches straight down to allow the head to slip through easily. Face the entire opening or bind with decorative braid or bias tape.

Next, hem the lower edges of the fabric so that it narrowly skims your instep.

Then, with wrong sides together and hems matching, diagonally seam from the outer hem on a 45-degree angle upward to within 12 inches of the shoulder fold. Repeat the seaming on the opposite corner, and your gown is complete, unless you want to embellish it with beading, decorative closures at the slashed neckline, or some other trim along the flowing sleeve edges.

Such "gowns" are appropriate for both male and female members of a Black Culture wedding and can be made to fit almost anyone by altering the angle of the single seam on each side.

Look like an angel . . .

3. If white on white *is* your thing, you can create an angelic gown of white drapery satin using nearly the same pattern as above. The look is all sweetness and light.

Purchase the same amount of material but begin with right sides together. Cut neck hole and slash, then create a V-neckline by folding the sides of the slash to the inside, pressing, to create an instant facing, then adding a bit of bias facing around the back to finish it off.

On the inside, stitch upward from the lower outside edge on a 45-degree angle to within 12 inches of the shoulder, then straight down to the hem. Repeat this seaming, clipping out the resulting wedge-shaped piece on either side. You may adjust size by varying the angle of either seam.

Then turn the material right side out and finish by trimming the neckline with white satin cording, as follows: Cut a piece of cording 4 yards long and fold it in half, placing the center at the back of the neckline. Hand-stitch around the neck edge, lapping one end over the other in front so that they can be crisscrossed around

the body to create a fitted bodice, tying at the waist. Place a half-knot about three inches from the bottom of each end of the cording, then create a tassel effect by combing the silk cord until it is fluffy, below the knot.

You may repeat the cording around the sleeve edges or finish them off with a hand-rolled hem, or sew lace binding on the inside.

Dress your attendants, male and female, in choir robes for a heavenly wedding at a miniprice.

No Sewing Needed

You can create an authentic Native American wedding dress without a sewing machine by using leather or vinyl.

A floor-length Indian gown will require about three yards of such fabric, a very sharp pair of scissors and a paper punch.

Fold the fabric in half crossways and lie down on it with your shoulders at the fold.

Stretch your arms out at shoulder level and have someone trace around you with a piece of chalk, leaving an inch-wide border along each side of your body, and marking neck and shoulder edges. You can try it first on butcher paper, if you like, and make a pattern.

Cut carefully along the chalk lines until you have a simple sleeveless floor-length shift with a fold at the shoulder. Make certain it will slip easily over the head.

Lap each side edge over the other one inch, and with a paper punch, make two rows of holes through the double thickness from under the arm to knee.

Using the long scraps left over when you cut the dress out, cut quarter-inch wide strips of the leather or vinyl and lace the shift together at each side.

Then with the sharpest scissors you can find, carefully fringe the bottom edge from hem to knee. (Unless you have a very good eye, it is best to mark the fringe line at half-inch intervals with chalk first.)

This is your basic gown. To make it an "original," select glass or wooden beads from the hobby shop and embroider them in simple designs around the neckline and bodice. An ambitious bride I recall even beaded each strip of fringe along the lower edge for a very elegant look.

Your gown may be either white or of a natural leather color, and the beading may be either monochromatic or multihued but the look will be poshly Pocahontas.

Table Lace Lovelies

You can create an almost "instant" wedding gown in minutes by simply selecting a large lace table cloth as the "yardage."

Depending upon your size and the length of gown you prefer (street length for an informal ceremony, ballerina length for an outdoor wedding, or floor length for a church wedding), select a lace table cloth that, when folded in half along its width with the fold at your shoulders, falls to the desired length.

A round or oval cloth is perfect. As most of these are self-bordered (some scalloped, others ruffled, or embroidered at the edges) there is very little sewing or hemming if you make your selection carefully.

To convert the cloth to a float-style gown, simply cut a hole in the center of the crosswise fold, large enough for your head, then cut a wedge-shaped piece about five inches wide at its base, approximately 15 to 20 inches down from the shoulder fold. Remove and save the wedge.

With right sides together, sew the resulting raw edges together to form the underarm and side seams of the gown. Then trim the neck hole with pieces of the lace (from the wedge you have cut away) or with a matching piece of satin, taffeta, or other suitable fabric. Wide satin ribbon can be used for this purpose, and a three-yard length folded in half can be used to form a stand-up collar in front and tied in a bow with trailing streamers at the neck back for a nice effect. Matching ribbon can be used to belt the float, or the dress can simply be allowed to skim the body (a nice design for the prominently pregnant bride.)

A peasant-style gown can be achieved by the same means, by simply enlarging the neck hole and hemming it, then running either a ribbon drawstring or elastic through the neckline. Take advantage of the self-trim of the sleeve edges by not hemming them at the very edge, but instead forming a casing two or three inches in from the edge and running elastic through it. This way you'll wind up with a ruffled sleeve that when pushed up to midforearm is pleasantly peasant and downright alluring.

To complete the peasant lace look, run an elastic casing slightly below waist level (to allow the top a slight blouson above the waist) and finish it off with ribbons tied at the waistline. Or belt the free-flowing gown with a peasant-style waist cincher of a solid color contrasting with the lace. Brown velvet is lovely with an ecru or beige lace gown like this.

You can use these same table cloth tricks to create your almost-instant attendants' dresses as well. Calico or gingham cloths are delightful with the peasant style, and pastel linen cloths look lovely with the float.

And, if you're really smart, you'll shop the white sales for the cloths for even extra savings!

By the way, as many cloths are also available as matching table ensembles that include runners and placemats, don't overlook this possibility for accessories to your gown and those of your attendants. Lace placemats can be easily fashioned into a variety of adorable headpieces for you and your attendants. Gathered around the edge and drawn up with ribbons or elastic, they form cute little Victorian bags that can be carried topped by a corsage instead of a bouquet. And folded in thirds they can be converted into clever clutch bags.

If you're feeling creative, buy several inexpensive placemats and play with them until you find a style that suits your needs. This way you can create some true originals on your own.

Lace runners are also fun to work with. Sewn to a length of ribbon, they make delightful aprons over skirts. Split, hemmed along the raw edges, and tied at the edges of the split with ribbons, they are attractive detachable collars. Folded lengthwise and sewn together with ribbons attached to the ends, they can become the waist cinches for peasant gowns. Or large, oval runners can even be converted into brief, mantilla-style veils of lace.

Spend some time in the linens department of your favorite department store, and you are bound to come away with even more ideas!

And if you are going to make your gown or your attendants' gowns, spend some time in the pattern books department of your fabric shop looking not in the formal and bridal sections, but in the loungewear and lingerie categories. These are much simpler patterns that even a nonsewer can use with little help, and they are adaptable to many theme weddings, including ethnic themes like Mexican, Hawaiian, and Oriental. Take a hint from the illustrations that follow, and you will find simple-to-sew styles that will turn you into a picture-pretty bride for pennies of what you expected to pay, even if you have to hire someone to do the sewing for you.

Accessories

All the savings made on your gown will be wasted if you indulge yourself at the bridal shop's accessory bar. A half-dozen "pretties" can cost you as much as you've budgeted for your whole ensemble.

But brides should be able to indulge themselves and to shop at length for just the right something to make them look unbelievably beautiful on their wedding day.

Penny-wise women today are shopping for ideas. They're looking beneath the fluff of the bridal boutique to see what those wedding-day dreams are made of—then putting it all together at home for a fraction of the retail price.

Wedding veils and headpieces are a prime example of the savings to be made. They range in price from $25 to $125 or more, depending on elaborateness of design. However, few of even the most exquisite are made up of more than $10 worth of materials and a few hours' time.

Keeping your wedding theme in mind, select a mood for your headpiece, then try on one of these tricks for size:

1. A charming way to top off a bridal ensemble with an heirloom look to it is to select your headdress from the baby bonnet bar of a ten-cent store or children's shop. You can find a wide variety of white lace ruffled bonnets on flexible straw bases in sizes meant to fit children up to six years of age. These are the kind popular at Easter or in the spring.

Because they are meant for a child's head, they will just fit across your crown (all that you desire for your purpose), and still allow enough room at the back to fasten a bouffant bit of veiling.

With three yards of silk illusion, the completed headpiece should cost less than $10, and a comparable one at a bridal shop would run about $30.

2. The floral supply houses that provide florists with the myriad ribbons, wires, and decorations used in making wedding and other floral arrangements can be a veritable playground for the creative bride.

With a $10 bill you can buy a variety of satin orange blossoms, ribbons, "pearl" hearts, silk leaves, and other motifs, as well as some white florists' tape and soft pliable wire to put them together. The possibilities are endless, as all manner of wreaths, tiaras, crowns and coronets can be put together and taken apart until just the right effect is achieved.

When you have the look you like, fill in the gaps with lots of tulle, then wire the whole thing to a clear plastic comb to insure anchoring it securely in your hair.

3. Dancers' supply stores or costume shops often sell starched muslin or wire bases for elaborate headdresses of other countries and other eras. These can be lavished with lace appliqués, embroidered with pearls and crystals for dramatic effect, or simply covered with fabric flowers attached with white glue.

One of the prettiest Camelot headdresses I have ever seen was made in less than an hour on such a base by a bride who clipped lace motifs from the scraps of her wedding gown to cover the base, then outlined the face-framing affair with seed pearl strings from the dime store. A few irridescent sequins for sparkle and she had an "original" to confine her floor-length veil. Total cost $5.75.

4. A romantic look borrowed from the Ukrainian peasants is the prettiest penny pincher I know. Instead of a veil, a spray of pastel flowers (either fresh or fabric) is fashioned to frame the face, then entwined with ribbons which are allowed to fall in mobile "ponytails" over the shoulders.

Using florists' ribbon of two or more colors and fabric flowers, a lavish look can be achieved for under $5.

5. Braiding fabric or fresh flowers and ribbons into the hair is also an inexpensive and effective bridal idea. If you have made a friend of your hairdresser in the past, she or he will want to do as much as possible for you on your wedding day, and if you supply the blooms and a bit of veiling or ribbon to experiment with beforehand, you can emerge from your shampoo and set all ready to step down the center aisle. This is a particularly pretty way to show off long hair on your wedding day.

For the *Love Story* look . . .

6. If you crochet or know someone who does, consider the *Love Story* look of the head-hugging Juliet caps made popular by actress Ali McGraw.

A beautiful bride I know made her own of white cotton string and crocheted in dime-store pearls and crystals for a dazzling effect that cost under $2.

She copied the pattern in pastel shades of yarn for her attendants, forsaking the jewels in favor of a single fabric daisy and a pair of floor-length streamers attached at the crown.

There were lots of other charming things about her wedding, but the caps were the sensation of the event, and all the more so because she had made them herself with love.

To make gorgeous garters . . .

7. The something blue of almost every bride is a blue garter, but in this carefree pantyhose generation the cost of these strictly decorative frills can be phenomenal. Still, you'll want one.

You can make your own for pennies, using two strips of two-inch wide blue satin ribbon, a length of $1^1/2$-inch elastic and a bit of lace edging.

Measure your leg just above the knee, then cut a piece of elastic two inches longer. Double that measurement for the ribbon and lace.

Cut both the ribbon and lace in half, then topstitch the two pieces of ribbon together lengthwise with right sides out, leaving the ends open. Stitch two rows of lace edging $1/2$ inch wide to the lower edge of the ribbon casing you have made.

Thread the elastic through and stitch the ends together. Slipstitch the raw ends of the ribbon under and finish the garter with a bow of half-inch white satin ribbon tied to a pair of dime-store wedding rings.

The whole thing will cost under $2 and comparable garters I have seen were priced up to $25.

Made in colors to match their gowns and minus the wedding rings, such garters are nice remembrances for the bridesmaids, too, and make pretty props for the photographer who likes a bit of cheesecake in the pre-wedding "candids."

Veils Are Easy

Veils come in a variety of lengths and styles, all easy to make in minutes, for a fraction of their cost over the counter.

For a floor-length veil that will sweep down the aisle behind you in romantic fashion, purchase four yards of silk or nylon illu-

sion. Fold the veiling lengthwise (it is usually 72 inches wide) and carefully cut it into two strips.

Fold the double thickness one-third down from the top and, using a covered white florist wire about 12 inches long, gather the veiling together at the fold with your fingers and secure it by winding the wire tightly around.

Attach the veiling to a clear plastic hair comb two or three inches wide, or directly to your headpiece. The shorter pieces can be folded forward to cover your face (forming a "blusher") as you approach the altar or left to fall free in back as an elbow-length tier.

Shorter veils can be created similarly by using multiple thicknesses to create a more bouffant effect. With four yards, an elbow-length veil has eight thicknesses and is created by folding the two four-yard strips in half and then in half again, gathering at the center fold and clipping the folded edges at the bottom.

Circular veils are pretty, too, and often trimmed with lace. Four yards of illusion is enough to create a pair of circles with 72-inch diameters.

Tack the circles together at the center, then sew on a comb underneath. Machine-stitch a lace border around each circle, finishing the ends carefully in back, and you have a hip-length veil that can be worn double thickness all around or off the face with four thicknesses in back.

A pretty variation of this veil is the mantilla look—a single lace-trimmed net (or all-lace) circle with the comb set about 6 inches back from one edge and the lace framing the face, while the remainder hangs in soft bias folds over the shoulders. A decorative Spanish comb to add height adds a dramatic look, too.

A circular veil 36 inches in diameter makes a pretty shoulder-length veil or brief mantilla. And 18-inch circles are just right for making bridesmaids' veils if you wish them.

For the Bridesmaids

Bridemaids' headpieces can be as simple or elegant as you like. A tailored bow with a hint of a veil is an ever popular style. A single fabric flower with a flutter of veiling to match the gowns is fast and pretty.

Whatever you select, however, keep in mind that the women will probably never wear them again, so it is foolish to spend too much on them.

I favor a garland of fresh flowers for spring weddings or a plastic headband covered with fabric or fur for fall.

You can do wonders with the scraps left over from the attendants' gowns. A peasant wedding gains a charming touch when bridesmaids wear tiny triangular scarfs tied under their chins. An African wedding looks more authentic with bridesmaids wearing triangular turbans. And you can create countless other headdresses from scraps, so before you toss them away take a second look.

With the same sort of florist wire that was used to gather the veil, bits of fabrics can be gathered into puff bows and attached to hair combs. To these can be added bits of satin or grosgrain ribbon streamers, and small fabric flowers to create a variety of looks suited to almost any wedding picture. The same sort of bows in bridal shops will cost up to $15 each, so it is well worth the time it takes to experiment a little with scraps before they go in the wastebasket.

Consider a clever crescent of silk flowers formed by simply twisting two strips of silk blossoms together at the ends and then separating them at the crown about four inches. On one side attach matching or contrasting ribbons and a single, larger silk flower of the same style, allowing the ribbons to flow in varying lengths to the shoulder.

The same effect can be achieved for a fall wedding by using silk leaves of fall hues and is a dramatic departure from the expected floral headpiece look.

"SHORTIE" PEASANT . AFRO

Or create fur caps in the same fashion by sewing two strips of fur together in the classic crescent and finishing at one side with a fur pompom.

A yard of "blusher" veiling (the kind used on women's hats to drop over the brim and sweep across the eyes) is also quite effective when simply swept over the face (from the nose up) and caught at the crown with a fabric flower, allowing the ends to float freely at the back of the head in a brief veil. This is an especially nice compliment to a bridal headpiece which uses the blusher on a hat in a similar manner. Only, in this case you simply forego the hat for the attendants, substituting a flower.

A bouffant bow of this type of veiling, attached to a simple barrette and clipped at the back of the head, is a romantic look as well. Or try using this versatile material to fashion your own fabric rose and dot it with two or three "diamond" dew drops that are affixed with white glue for a bit of sparkle.

Keep it simple and you'll keep the costs down while you insure good taste. You don't want your attendants to be so elaborate that they'll detract from your own moment of glamour.

A Checklist for the Home-Sewn Bridal Ensemble and Seamstress

1. *Purchase all needed materials at the same time!* Dye lots differ, and the only way to insure a perfect match of fabric is to get it from the same bolt or dye lot. The same fabric from the same mill may differ significantly in color from one lot to another, so be sure to buy enough the first time to avoid obvious color variations in your gown or the gowns of your attendants.

2. *Follow pattern guidelines in selecting fabrics.* The advice on pattern covers is the advice of experts. A design perfect for taffeta or peau de soie may fall flat in voile or organdy! A gown with drapes and bias cut sleeves or skirt won't work in material that has too much substance, so be sure to use something more supple, like crepe or georgette.

3. *Don't wait until the last minute!* Even if you are adept at whipping up a perfect ensemble overnight, don't wait until the last minute to make your wedding gown. Some fabrics have to be ordered special. Bridal gowns need careful fitting and finishing to look picture perfect. These things take time. Allow yourself as much lead time as possible if you are going to be making your own gown or having it made.

4. *Make comfort a top consideration!* You will be wearing your bridal gown all day and well into the evening if you are having a large wedding and reception. Make sure the style is easy to wear and won't interfere with your planned activities. For example, a 10-foot train may look lovely walking down the aisle, but do you want to dance at your reception? Then consider a detachable train, or one you can bustle-up with a bow or hook after the ceremony. Otherwise, you'll have it draped over your arm all during the reception.

Likewise, voluminous sleeves may make for pretty pictures but don't look well after being dipped into your bridal dinner. If you'll be eating in your gown, consider the difficulty of managing this normally easy activity in your chosen design.

And if the weather will be extremely hot or cold, select your gown and fabric accordingly. You'll want to look and feel fresh all day.

5. *Hem CAREFULLY! Buy your wedding shoes BEFORE you hem your dress.* A gown that is an inch too long or too short not only can ruin the total look you are trying to achieve but also can be a hazard to navigation as well. Purchase your wedding shoes before you hem your gown and wear them while the hem is being pinned in place. Double-check the length with petticoats in place to make sure you'll be able to navigate the center aisle with ease and trip the light fantastic at the reception without tripping on your hem somewhere along the way!

6. *Give the gowns a backward glance.* Unless you'll be facing the guests at your wedding (a relatively new option), be sure your gown and those of your attendants have some significant back interest. A pretty sash that falls from the waist at back, a lace panel, a ruffled train, a long veil, or some other back interest should be sewn into your gowns so they'll look just as lovely from the back as they do from the front.

7. *Place lace carefully before you cut it!* The loveliest of lace can look shabby unless carefully cut. The patterns worked into the lace should be placed carefully for the maximum effect when cutting your gown. This is particularly true if your lace has large floral motifs or vertical stripes. Be sure they are going in the right direction, are centered when appropriate, and so on. Treat lace as if it were a napped fabric and allow enough extra material for perfect placement of the motifs.

8. *If you select a bordered fabric (particularly eyelet) be sure to allow extra fabric.* Bordered materials, such as some laces with scalloped edges and eyelets with border patterns, require some careful cutting and additional fabric requirements. You won't save any money if you skimp here! Consult the fabric salesperson for correct yardage requirements and then buy enough extra to allow for any possible mistakes.

9. *Keep it SIMPLE!* If in doubt about how far to go in your bridal design, or those for your attendants and mothers, it is far better to err on the side of simplicity than to overdo it. I have seen otherwise beautiful weddings spoiled by too many sequins, rhinestones, and ruffles. Remember, a touch is never too much. Don't overdo anything—particularly when it comes to necklines that are revealing or fabrics that are quite sheer. *If in doubt, throw it out* is a good rule.

10. *Consider your jewelry when making or designing your dress.* Unless you are a member of the Royal Family, forget huge necklaces, long drop earrings, and diamond tiaras! But if you will be wearing a gift of jewelry from your husband-to-be, your mother, grandmother, or someone else, consider how it will look with your gown before you make your final selection. A pearl choker is lovely with a scooped neckline but gets lost in a ruffled collar. A diamond brooch must be pinned someplace, so if you are planning to wear one, don't select an off-the-shoulder gown with no place to put it. You get the idea!

11. *Consider the age and size of your attendants and family when selecting gowns for those who will be part of the wedding party.* If you are over forty, don't select a teenage prom style wedding gown, no matter how much you love it. Choose a dress appropriate to your age and size. This goes for your attendants and family as well. Nothing spoils a wedding like a full-sized maid of honor stuffed into a fitted gown or a petite bride lost in a gown that is overpowering. If you are unsure, have those who will be wearing the gowns you're making try on similar styles available in ready-to-wear. If you don't know the taste of your mother or mother-in-law to be, cut out pictures you like or feel are appropriate for them and send them along with a note saying you think they'd look "perfect" in something of the sort. Or ask if you can tag along when they go shopping or selecting patterns.

I attended a perfectly beautiful afternoon garden wedding recently where the mother of the groom showed up looking for all the world as if she'd just stepped out of a bordello, in an evening gown that Mae West wouldn't have worn in her worst movie (too tight, too low cut, too many sequins and rhinestones, and totally inappropriate to the outdoor afternoon setting). I don't think anyone even saw the bride! All eyes were on the person who had chosen red satin and spangles for the occasion and seemed to be wearing the crown jewels on top of it!

If you're afraid this could happen to you, offer to make the gown yourself or to have it made. Or get someone to talk to the "wild one" well in advance.

12. *Consider your lingerie carefully as you make your gowns.* Flash bulbs will be popping at you all day, and you wouldn't have it any other way. We all want photographic portraits to cherish. But flash equipment can perform magic on some fabrics. I've seen more than one set of wedding photos where the bride or one of her attendants seemed to be wrapped in cellophane rather than chiffon or lace! Make sure your under garments are opaque! A full slip the length of all gowns or a heavy lining is a must, particularly if you'll be outside with the sun at your back! Imagine the horror of one bride I know when she saw that her gown became transparent under the powerful strobe light used by her photographer.

So hold your fabric and lining up to strong lights before you buy them, and if they are the least bit transparent, plan on extra undergarments!

9
fun flowers
and un-flowers

Unless your father's hobby is raising hothouse orchids or Aunt Fanny is a florist, flowers for your wedding can be a major expense.

Substantial savings can be made by cutting down on the amount of flowers and the kind of arrangements. But don't let the savings be made at the expense of a picture-pretty ceremony.

There was a time when unless the church was filled to overflowing with baskets and bowers of flowers, no self-respecting bride would step down the center aisle. That time has passed. Today's brides are turning their backs on the huge quantities of flowers favored by their mothers and selecting, instead, more romantic and ingenious floral fancies.

Changing Trends

Church decorations, at one time traditionally white wicker baskets of fragrant blooms (and the more the better), are now frequently far more understated—with evergreens, ivy, and fern often completely replacing flowers at the altar.

Candles, more in vogue now than for many years, are also replacing or cutting down on the number of flowers used to adorn the church.

A brace of floor-standing candelabras, each holding eight tall white candles, can be festooned with evergreen or fern garlands for a fraction of the cost of a pair of flower-filled baskets, and is far more romantic looking.

An altar laden with greens and featuring an elegant white wicker birdcage with a pair of doves inside was the dramatic decoration chosen by the daughter of a friend of mine who was married last year in Washington, D.C. Both the birds and the cage were borrowed and didn't add a cent to the wedding expenses but added immeasurably to the ceremony, leaving guests with a topic of conversation throughout the reception and for weeks afterward.

Creative artistry such as this can also be applied to the bride's flowers and to those of her wedding party with spectacular results both in looks and in savings.

Super Savings

One of the most impressive ceremonies I ever attended was a summer wedding in New Orleans where the bride traded the traditional bouquet for a white lace fan with a single gardenia fastened to it with satin streamers. Pale pink camellias attached to deep pink paper fans were carried by the attendants, creating a pretty picture of plantation house elegance at the altar.

The Christmas wedding of a friend in New York a few years ago featured a similar idea, with bride and attendants carrying white fur muffs. The bride's was adorned with a corsage of white roses and holly, and the attendants' featured holly sprigs and red streamers.

Both of these brides let the themes of their weddings suggest substitutes for the normal floral pieces and, while saving money, left a lasting impression of ingenuity on their guests.

Given $100 by her father to purchase flowers for her wedding, one bride I recall blew half of it on a tall antique candelabra with tinkling crystal prisms. She used it as the focal point of church decorations in place of a flower arrangement, and long after the altar decor of friends' weddings had been forgotten, she was still using it as a table centerpiece at special dinner parties.

Lei It On

A bride whose father actually did raise hothouse orchids as a hobby used the exotic blooms lavishly in a wedding with a traditional Polynesian flavor.

Selecting dozens of baby vanda orchids from her father's hothouse, the bride strung them together with needle and thread to make island leis for her bridesmaids, ushers, and groom to wear during the ceremony.

Making orchid, plumeria, or carnation leis is no more difficult than stringing beads. Begin with some heavy thread, a needle with a large eye, and a good supply of fresh flowers.

A box of soda straws will help you work faster and cut the number of flowers used substantially. Snip each straw into one-inch lengths and use the small pieces as spacers, positioning them between each bloom. Select paper or plastic straws in colors similar to the flowers you have chosen so that they will be as unobtrusive as possible.

Thread the needle, doubling the heavy thread, and making a large knot at the end. The thread should be about three inches longer than you want the lei to be and the lei should be large enough to slip on and off over the head easily.

Now begin by threading first a flower, then a soda straw spacer and repeat, being careful to handle the flowers as little as possible and to thread them at dead center from front to back. Orchids may look better without the spacers, but this will require double the amount. Plumeria looks lovely with the spacers, which fit over the small stems at the flower's base.

Carnations are done in the same way—first a flower, then a straw, and so on. Once you have completed a string of the carnations, however, go back and carefully strip away the green bud portion beneath the bloom and gently shake or fluff the foliage of the flower's head until the lei grows fluffy and round, hiding the soda straw spacers beneath a mane of fragrant petals.

If you have never made leis before, it is best to experiment ahead of time to get the feel of the operation. Though it is simple, you must work quickly and in a cool place, putting each finished lei in a plastic bag with a bit of moisture and storing it in the refrigerator until the wedding.

These may be made up a day or two in advance, but never more. It is best, if possible, to have helpers put them together the day of the wedding, but if that is not possible, the night before is all right.

The use of the lei in a Hawaiian style wedding can take many forms. All attendants, as well as the bride and groom, may wear them around their necks. But even if you make them at home this can be quite expensive.

The bride and groom can be the only two to wear full leis, however, with the attendants wearing smaller versions encircling their heads. This is equally as effective at a fraction of the cost.

Still another variation of the use of the floral lei is to have each woman in the wedding party wear a small lei or flowers in her hair and carry a large neck lei in her hands as she steps down the aisle, giving it to her male counterpart as she reaches the altar.

Though leis are traditionally given with a kiss, that custom is foregone here, with each bridesmaid simply placing the lei around the usher's neck, then stepping aside to her place at the left of the altar. Only the bride does not give her floral offering to the groom at this point in the ceremony.

She continues to hold the wreath as she would a bouquet until the minister asks the couple to join hands, after her father has given her in marriage.

At this time she places the lei around the groom's neck and the couple recite their vows. When they have been pronounced husband and wife, and the exchange of rings is complete, the groom returns the lei to his bride with a kiss.

Simple Elegance

Flowers for your wedding don't have to be as exotic as these island blooms. They can be impressive in other ways.

The simple elegance of a prayer book topped by a single long-stemmed rose and a spray of heather fern is a very dramatic way to keep costs low.

You'll look like an angel stepping to the altar with this arrangement in hand, and your attendants can forego flowers completely and carry, instead, lighted tapers with satin streamers, either placing them one at a time in candelabras at the front of the church or continuing to hold them throughout the service, standing in a semicircle behind the minister rather than all at one side as is usual.

Musical Flowers?

Small glass wind chimes, the kind you find in Chinatown, hand-painted with delicate floral motifs, can be purchased for about $1 each in specialty shops, dime stores or garden shops.

These can be used with a single gardenia, orchid, or other large flower to create a carrying piece that rivals any bouquet you might order from a florist.

Using florist tape (the stretchy green or white inexpensive tape found at most variety stores or florist supply houses), fasten the flower and some ribbons to the top of the wind chimes so that

WIND CHIMES

you can still clasp your fingers through the strings behind it as though in prayer.

This way the chimes will hang below your clasped hands, and the gardenia or other flowers will be held just in front of your fingers.

A bonus here is the ethereal music created as your attendants step ahead of you to the altar. Even your quaking knees will add a musical tinkle to the ceremony that will be a sheer delight to those witnessing the ceremony. This idea is particularly suited to either Hawaiian-, Chinese- or Japanese-inspired ceremonies or garden weddings.

Leave the Stems On

For a fresh young look, carry a presentation style bouquet of white and yellow daisies and baby's breath instead of the formal bridal bouquet.

This is really nothing more than a large bunch of flowers with the stems and foliage left on. Arrange them in layers with those having the longest stems on the bottom and the shorter stems on top until you have a pleasant-looking armful.

Secure them with florist tape by wrapping the stems about three inches up from the base, then covering the wrapped area with satin ribbons or a large bow.

Carry them in your right arm as you step to the altar with your father on your left. You'll look as if you just stepped from a famous painting by one of the old masters, particularly if you have selected a peasant style gown or one of Renaissance styling.

Christmas Glamour

For a Christmas wedding, make wreaths of holly or poinsettias and evergreens for your attendants to carry by attaching the greens and flowers to a styrofoam circle with florist wire and the pointed wooden picks (flora-picks) you can buy for pennies at a florist supply house. These are easily carried if a covered wire handle is attached to the back on each side, and they make excellent decorations at the reception later.

Your own flowers can be done in the same fashion, but you may want to make your wreath of Mystery gardenias and shiny lemon leaves for contrast.

Wreaths done in multicolored spring flowers are also charming for both bridesmaids and bride. These can be interspersed with ribbons and feature floor-scraping streamers for a touch of the European peasant look.

If this is the look you like, carry it a step further and make daisy chains for your attendants to wear in their hair and fashion a Ukranian peasant headdress for yourself by wiring flowers like those of your bridal bouquet together to form a coronet framing the face. Then attach bunches of ribbons to fill in the gaps and yard-long bunches of streamers at each temple to fall in mobile "pony-tails" over the shoulders.

To make the coronet, begin by selecting a dozen small blooms —daisies, bachelor buttons, small mums of varying hues, roses and baby's breath make a nice assortment—then clip their stems to about one inch each.

Fasten a three- or four-inch piece of light gauge florist wire to each stem by inserting the wire into the base of the bloom alongside the stem, then wrap them tightly with florist tape.

Once the individual flowers are prepared, you can mix and match them as you like by bending the wires together until you achieve a pleasing, face-framing arrangement. When that is done, fill in with ribbons and add streamers as stated above.

For Good Luck

Ivy, the traditional good luck green for brides, is inexpensive and can be used to create a pretty bouquet with just a few flowers. A styrofoam base, either a sphere, cone or crescent, is a good way to start.

Attach sprigs of the greenery to the base, using the flora-pick method until the base is covered completely. Then, with the ivy as a backdrop, add colorful blooms here and there until the desired effect is achieved.

Colored or white net (available at only pennies per yard) can be used similarly to form a background and hide a bouquet base. The net can be gathered in small bunches and attached to the foam base with florist pins. These bases can be made up far in advance and the fresh flowers added the day of the wedding.

If you want to save more time than money in creating such an arrangement, tulle balls or puffs can be purchased in the housewares departments of many major markets and department stores. Used for dishwashing, they are nonetheless colorfully attractive and when attached to a foam base with pins, create a frilly background in which to nestle individual flowers. A particularly pretty look that can be created in this manner is the topiary ball.

Begin by covering a three-inch styrofoam ball with the tulle puffs. Attach a length of two-inch wide ribbon, 12 inches long, to the top of the ball with florist pins. Double the ribbon so it forms a loop you can easily slip your fingers through. Add a doubled streamer of the same ribbon at the opposite or bottom side of the ball and you have a piece that can be carried by clasping the hands through the top loop.

To finish these unique bouquets—if they can be called that— add tiny sprigs of the ribbon here and there and at the last minute poke in a dozen or so fresh flowers of a matching or contrasting shade, using the flora-pick method.

Cage Your Flowers

An artful carrying-piece for bridesmaids that almost does away with flowers completely, yet is perfect for a garden wedding or spring ceremony, is the birdcage bouquet.

Tiny wicker birdcages—the kind never meant to confine a bird—are lavished with satin streamers and feature a single, full-blow rose, camellia, or gardenia trapped inside.

The cages can be used in the natural wicker or rattan color or sprayed to match the bridesmaids' gowns.

To carry out the springtime themes, select a nosegay of bright spring flowers and top it off with a lifelike feather butterfly available at florist or specialty shops.

To fashion an old-fashioned nosegay, purchase a plastic base with lace paper liner from the floral supply house, then select flowers either from your own garden or from the florist and arrange them inside. Finish the old-fashioned look with lots of ribbons and slim satin streamers tied in love knots.

Carry a Parasol

Instead of a traditional bouquet base, a paper parasol can be trimmed with flowers and lace to make a pretty carrying-piece.

If the wedding is to be outdoors, have the bridesmaids carry the parasols over their shoulders with a bunch of violets at the tops and streamers trailing in the wind.

If the wedding is to take place indoors, the parasols may be carried either fully closed with a garland of ivy and flowers wound around the closed cone, or partially opened with a spray of flowers or corsage pinned on. This is a million-dollar look for pennies, with a richly romantic mood.

PARASOL

Love Lights

Candles, if permitted in your church or other wedding site, are an elegant substitute for costly flowers and add a warmth and charm that enhance any evening ceremony.

But you must be careful with the lighted candles—particularly around veils and diaphanous dresses.

What to do? Consider captive candles for both charm and safety.

A glowing votive candle in a colored glass cup, trapped inside a tiny antique-looking lantern, is a charming carrying piece for bridesmaids, in lieu of a mundane bouquet. Top the inexpensive lanterns with bows and greenery for a finishing touch that will be the envy of the fanciest florist.

You'll find lanterns that are appropriate for this use in the candle departments of major chain stores, in hardware and even sporting goods stores. Shop around for a shape and price that you like, but don't worry about the color. A red, railroad lantern looks lovely sprayed in a soft pastel color and many of the lanterns are already an antiqued brass, copper, or silver color that is completely appropriate to a wedding.

When the wedding is over, these can become the bridesmaids' gifts, as they are everlasting remembrances of your attendants' participation in your special day. So consider the cost of these lanterns as replacing both a bouquet and a memento for your bridesmaids.

A hurricane lamp is also a safe and sane way of using candles in place of flowers. And there are many varieties available in the glassware departments of department stores, garden shops, and import stores.

If you find these too expensive for your budget, consider creating your own hurricane lamps by converting an inexpensive glass tumbler into a candle chimney.

For example, select a hollow-stemmed champagne glass and insert a slim taper into the stem. Tie the stem with ribbons, a bit of baby's breath, or fern for an elegant effect.

Almost any shapely glass can be used in this way. The best are tall enough to enclose the candle completely and tapered toward the bottom, or bowed in the middle for easy and safe carrying.

To affix the candle securely, you need only place a small piece of florist's clay to the bottom of the candle and press it into the bottom of the glass. You can hide the clay cleverly by pouring about an inch of fragrant potpourri into the bottom after the candle is in place, or by inserting some silk flowers into the clay at the base of the candle before you fasten it to the glass.

Again, ribbons, some fern, or baby's breath tied to the outside of the glass makes a festive finishing touch to your hurricane lamps.

And these lamps are just as lovely in a church that is softly lighted during the day as in the evening—or used outside at an early morning or evening ceremony, provided that it is not too windy for safety.

Forget the Flowers Entirely

You can do away with floral pieces for your attendants completely, and not sacrifice a beautiful look a bit, if you present them each with a pair of white cotton gloves and an inexpensive prayer book to be covered in fabric that matches their dresses.

White-gloved girls carrying tiny prayer books covered in soft hues are a charming sight. If you still want flowers, create halos of baby rosebuds and baby's breath for a truly angelic look. These are made in the manner of the Ukrainian headpiece on page 85, but rather than a face-framing shape, a circle is formed with streamers trailing down the back. Or omit the streamers completely if you wish.

You can echo this angelic look by carrying a white Bible covered in fabric left over from your dress. Pin on a single orchid or a gardenia corsage to wear at the reception later.

Attach three yards of white tulle to the rear of your floral halo, to trail over your train or to replace it entirely. Intersperse it with ribbons for a fabulous look.

Finally, for a turn-of-the-century wedding, have attendants carry small evening bags, either the satin or crepe drawstring variety or the tiny pouches with sparkly chain handles, and pin a bunch of violets or a camellia to each.

You might select a lace fan with just a flower or two pinned to the base or a lace and satin muff with a corsage pinned on.

Double Your Pleasure

Many of these floral fancies can double as decorations at the reception if you plan wisely. The tiny birdcages hanging from an ivy-covered arbor are a charming sight at a garden reception, for example.

The topiary balls hang nicely indoors, or out, and the fragrant Hawaiian leis are beautiful additions to the refreshment table, framing the punch bowl or wedding cake base for an authentic island touch.

Whatever you select in the way of flowers, don't be afraid to do it yourself, for these simple ideas can easily be put together by a beginner and, if you employ members of the family or wedding party, will go together in no time.

Make a Friend of the Florist

If you just want to borrow these ideas and have a florist make them up, you won't save as much money but you'll still be a smashingly beautiful bride.

And for those who will go this route, here are a few handy hints on selecting a florist. First, do some comparative shopping by phone to find out the relative costs of the ideas you favor. When you find a florist within your range, plan a visit at a time that is convenient for him or her and sit down and discuss in detail what you want and how much you have to spend.

A deposit will probably be required if your order is a large one, so you should plan to bring your checkbook along.

Use the same technique when you make a friend of your photographer. Share your enthusiasm for your plans and you may find this "artist" will surprise you pleasantly, too!

If you promise the florist a photo to display in the shop after the wedding, you may be overwhelmed!

Most florists give their artistic all to make their brides beautiful, but few ever get to see the total effect of their work unless the client happens to be a relative. If you give your florist one of the inexpensive prints of your wedding party to use as a sales piece later, she or he will thank you for it with more than just words.

10
picture this

Every bride agrees that her wedding pictures are priceless mementos of a very special time. Relying on this feeling, studio photographers have turned wedding photography into a multimillion dollar business, worldwide.

While few small-town photographers get rich from the weddings they shoot, many a photo studio owner relies on brides for his or her bread and butter, knowing that professional photo work is as important to most weddings as flowers and a cake.

Hiring a photographer for a wedding is like selecting a family doctor. You want a professional, because if things aren't done right the first time, there may not be another chance. Still, there are professionals and *professionals*.

If money is no object and if you have no real preference as to the kind of wedding photos you would like (except that they be first quality prints) then a studio photographer would be your choice. He or she will offer you a selection of "package plans," usually beginning at about $50 for the shooting and your choice of a dozen 8 × 10's in black and white. The bill can be as much as $300 for the same number of color prints in a wedding album, however. Wallet-sized photos, outsized enlargements, special toning, tinting, or textured paper finishes will all be extra and can double the bill or even triple it, depending on how many poses you select and how many prints you desire of each.

Contract for Photos Only

If you select a studio photographer for your wedding, here are some hints to insure getting the most for the least.

Contract for photos alone. A fancy album can always be purchased at a later date when there aren't so many other places for Dad and Mom's money to go.

Settle on a price in advance for the shooting and a minimum number of prints, then get it in writing!

Make certain your studio also gives you written notice of how much additional prints will be and the option to purchase them at any time up to a year after your wedding date. Most studios keep negatives on file for at least that long, but many will try to pressure you into buying more than you can afford in the beginning by making it seem like a once-in-a-lifetime opportunity. In reality, it is simply easier for them to do all your work at once.

Finally, arrange with your photographer for an advance sitting and black and white glossy prints to be distributed to the local

newspapers. Many studios will throw this into the package if you demand it, but few will offer it free unless you do.

Pros, Not Cons

Studio photographers are not the only professionals willing and able to shoot weddings and produce high quality prints, however. There are many other working "pros" in even small towns who moonlight by taking wedding pictures. Because it is their second job, they will usually do your work at a substantial reduction in rates.

Newspaper photographers, police photographers, industrial camera operators, members of college and university newspaper and yearbook staffs all are capable of producing the kind of professional quality you can rely on, and in many instances will actually give you better pictures because they aren't tied to studio concepts of what wedding photos should look like.

Often, too, they are far more anxious to please than the studio pro who "has shooting weddings down to a science," which usually means a set number of poses that take the least time and effort.

You Get What You Pay For

One bride I knew who was married in the formal garden of her family's Virginia estate was crushed when the studio photographer she had hired at considerable expense declared the outdoor setting "far too informal" for wedding portraits and marched her wedding party inside to shoot them, like prisoners before a firing squad, against a blank wall.

Equally as unhappy, however, was the Massachusetts Miss who thought she was getting a bargain by hiring a photo-hobbyist friend to shoot her wedding for only the cost of materials. He took all the desired shots and bent over backwards to please, but when the couple returned from their honeymoon expecting to view proofs of his splendid work, he had only his own red face to show them.

With exuberance over his photographic triumph, he had hastened to his darkroom in the wee hours after the reception and

there mistook fixer for developer, ruining the five rolls of film he
had shot with such expertise.

The point is you get what you pay for but don't necessarily
have to pay through the nose!

Communicate!

Whomever you select to record your wedding on film, make a friend
of her or him. Sit down and chat about the sort of wedding it will be.
Let the photographer know in advance if there are to be special moments in the ceremony you will particularly want photos of, and
give her or him a chance to get to know you and the kind of pictures
that will really turn you on. You may be surprised at how turned on
your photographer will get at shooting a wedding that isn't just the
same ritual he or she has performed a dozen times before.

One young couple who really conveyed their wedding plans to
their photographer with feeling, had him asking them to "allow"
him to do some special darkroom work with their photos and for
their "permission" to have the pictures entered in a photo contest
he was going to compete in soon.

The results were a spectacular set of "superimpositions"
which genuinely conveyed the dreamlike quality the wedding day
had for the couple. One shot of them kneeling together at the altar
was superimposed on an ocean sunset scene for a beautiful post-
script to their wedding collection and a first prize ribbon for the
photographer at the fair.

You may not be this lucky, but if you convey your excitement
and enthusiasm to your photographer, letting him know you have
chosen him because you are certain he is the only one who can picture the festivities the way you really want to remember them,
you'll be sure to get his best work.

Ask for Samples

Don't be afraid to ask to see a portfolio of the work your photographer has done. And when you have seen it, if you aren't genuinely

pleased, don't be afraid to look elsewhere. Any photographer worth his Kodabromide-F will have a stack of photos he or she has been waiting to show anyone who will sit still long enough to look.

If you like the work, show your enthusiasm. Point out any photos that are in line with those you would like to have made and jot down any ideas you may get from what the photographer has to show you. Be aware that photographers generally consider themselves artists and react in kind. A little praise goes a long way toward inspiring them to new heights.

Color?

A decision that must be made almost as soon as the photographer is selected is, will the photos be in color or will they be the far less expensive black and white. Cost is not the only factor to consider here.

Black and white photos are less expensive, but they are actually much more versatile than color. First, and possibly most important, they can be easily retouched if needed. They can be toned, tinted, antiqued, printed through textured screens, as "sand-

wiched" double exposures for special effects, or on a wide variety of papers that give everything from pronounced textures to subtle pearlescent tones. And of course they can be tinted with photo oils for a colored effect, or made into an oil portrait at a later date, if you like.

Color photos have the obvious advantage of being natural looking in every way. They are more expensive, to be sure, but if you know a few tricks of the trade they may not be so much more that you should have to do without them if you really want color.

A studio may charge as much as $35 for a single 8 × 10 natural color portrait of the bride, as opposed to about $7.50 for one in black and white.

If, however, you shoot a roll of color film yourself and have an 8 × 10 print made at the corner drugstore, you will find that the color enlargement will be only about $6. What is the difference? The photographer's time, mostly. If he or she has to set up enlarger and color apparatus just for your single-print order, the cost will naturally be high. So if you want color you get the best price by agreeing in advance to a dozen or more prints. At that number, you should get a substantial break in price per unit.

Try This

Another idea to consider, if you are dead set on color, is to hire a photographer to do only the shooting, giving you the undeveloped film to be processed and printed by a mass production firm. Some photographers will balk at this idea (and studios won't hear of it), but it can save you a substantial amount of money and you will still get professional results, if you can find a pro who'll agree.

Many nationwide firms deal in color processing by mail. Through mass production techniques their prices are quite low, and because a good deal of the work is automated, the quality is generally high, or at least better than average. Prints are usually uniform in tone and will measure up nicely against those done individually even by a seasoned veteran.

If this sounds good to you, it will sound even better when you hear that the cost per 8 × 10 print can drop as low as $2 each if you do some comparative shopping in advance.

Do Some Shopping

Scan the advertisements in the major photo magazines. You will find numerous companies specializing in color printing and enlargement. Shoot a roll of color film yourself, or have someone who knows the shutter from the lens of a camera do it for you, then mail your "test roll" to firm "A" for developing and printing. Most of these firms will send you a free roll of film along with your prints, so all you are risking is the price of developing (about $3 by mail order) and if your test roll is snapshots you've taken at a shower or engagement party, you won't be losing a thing.

Once you receive your prints through the mail you will be able to judge the quality of the work and decide whether or not you would trust your wedding order to them. If you think it is worthy, go one step further and select a sample print to be enlarged, send it in and again appraise the quality on its return.

This type of testing takes times (usually at least a week for each order), so plan ahead if you want to go this route. And don't give up if the first company isn't up to your standards. Try again if you have the time, remembering that the savings could be substantial!

Mass Production

Whether or not you select color, the mass production companies you will find advertised in the major photo magazines can be used to augment your wedding photo order. Most offer quantity orders at pennies per print, so once you have your wedding pictures in hand, select one you would like to send to friends or relatives in distant cities and splurge on a mass order of your favorite print, via mail.

You can have 20 or more wallet-sized color prints made for about 25 cents each from at least a dozen firms across the country. Mounted 5 × 7 color prints (ideal gifts for members of the wedding party) can be ordered similarly for about $.50 each, in batches of ten or more, from a single print or transparency. And 8 × 10's, ordered ten at a time from a single pose, run about $2 each.

Everyone has seen magazine ads offering black and white wallet-sized photos, 12 for $1. These are ideal for enclosing with thank-you notes, and if you send off your favorite shot right away, you'll have them back to enclose before you are finished writing your thank-you's.

Black and white enlargements via mail can be found in penny-wise packages, too, like three 5 × 7's for $5; two 8 × 10's and four 5 × 7's for $10, or myriad other inexpensive combinations. All of these can be ordered without a negative by simply sending in your original print, which is returned, unharmed, with your order.

There are seldom more than one or two shots out of a whole wedding that you would want many extra copies of, so before you put Mama and Papa in the poor house with huge orders from the photographer, consider limiting yourself to one shot you like, and getting additional prints this way. Some of these companies even offer additional heavyweight papers and sepia toning at no additional cost.

You can have spectacular wedding pictures and skip the cost of a photographer altogether. In fact, you can even skip the cost of film.

A very creative couple of my acquaintance hired a courtroom illustrator to record their wedding and wound up with a book of pictures that is the envy of everyone who has seen it.

Fast and accurate, these "jiffy" artists are used to catching the action as it comes—they capture the moment, with all the emotion it contains.

You've seen their drawings. They are the ones on television news. Imagine that kind of art work in your wedding album. My friends paid about half what they had allotted for photographs to hire the artist. And the results were many times more impressive than the standard wedding photos.

When they were through, they had "instant" pictures to show at the reception where all the wedding guests could enjoy them. Later they selected their favorite sketch and commissioned the artist to do a large portrait, which now proudly graces their fireplace wall.

You can contact such artists by calling your local television station or network affiliate.

Or talk to the art professors at your community college or university. They can usually recommend a talented student with the right skills who could use some extra money. There may even be someone in your own family who is a whiz at such drawings and would be happy to gift you with a set.

The instant photo is a good adjunct to your primary wedding pictures, too. A thoughtful friend of my daughter carries her Polaroid camera along to every wedding she attends and makes up her wedding gift throughout the day.

With a prepurchased photo album that she had gold-stamped with the names of the couple in advance, she snaps happily away during the ceremony and reception, placing the photos one by one in the album throughout the day. Before departing she gives the filled album to the lucky couple to enjoy on their honeymoon.

Her thoughtfulness actually saved one bride's day. For while the professional photographer's work was ruined in a darkroom accident, the couple still had a record of their wedding to cherish forever more.

Accessories

There are dozens of photo accessories you may want, or be tempted to buy on impulse, when placing your wedding order. Albums are the most costly, and although they are convenient and attractive, they are not an immediate necessity. The cost of a leather-bound, engraved, photo book with plastic pages in which to display your wedding pictures can double the cost of your photography bill if you buy it from a photo studio. They are about a third less direct from a stationer's or a bookshop. Regular photo albums (the nonwedding variety) are less than half the price and a far better buy.

If your Aunt Minnie sends you a check you simply don't know what to do with, and you decide to spend it on an album for your photos, I suggest one of the multipurpose affairs. These are not just photo albums but actually wedding diaries of a sort.

Put out by several of the top greeting card manufacturers, these albums may include—in addition to photo sections—the traditional wedding guest register (which you'll plan to purchase anyway), a gift register, a thank-you note check list, a record of showers and other social events, handy pockets for keepsakes (your garter and the sixpence from your shoe, for example), space for snapshots, a record of your honeymoon journey, and sometimes even space for a bit about your first apartment or home. All of this costs about the same price you'd pay for a comparable wedding album alone, and most are attractively bound in vinyl or fabric and enhanced with artwork and poetry inside.

Other photographic accessories you may want—frames, presentation folders, and the like—are also better purchased outside the photo studio or from someone other than the photographer. Not only will the prices be better from a department store, or specialty shop, but the selection will be wider as well.

If you have a "crafty" nature or know someone who does, you may want to invest some time rather than money in your photo accessories.

The nostalgic quilted albums of lace, lavished with ruffles and satin ribbons, embroidery or counted cross stitch are as easy to whip up as a pillow. They do take some time, and depending upon the lavishness of the design, some careful handwork, but they are well worth the effort.

You can buy them in elite country boutiques, but they are quite expensive. If you are clever, you'll look them over and copy the one you like best, using scraps from your wedding dress to make the album jacket even more meaningful.

Patterns are available from most yardage stores or crafts catalogues. And, some of the larger crafts shops or needlework shops offer classes for the bride-to-be, where these books are one of the major projects.

Imagine a lovely lace album, to display on your coffee table alongside a matching quilted frame holding your wedding portrait. Wouldn't you be proud to tell everyone who admires them that you made them yourself?

The quilted frames are also lovely remembrances for members of your bridal party, particularly when they are handmade by the bride.

Another nice way to display some wedding photos and mementos (such as imprinted matches, napkins, dried flowers from your bouquet, and other wedding treasures) is in a shadow-box frame to hang on the wall.

These unfinished frames are available inexpensively at most craft and collectable stores. They are $1^1/2$ to 2" deep frames with small wooden compartments behind the glass.

You can stain or varnish them to match your decor before the wedding and afterward you can have fun arranging special photos, your wedding invitation, the bride and groom from your cake, and more under glass to preserve them as family heirlooms.

I suggested this idea to a friend several years ago, and she followed through. When the shadow box was complete, she was so pleased that she has continued the idea, making one for each of her children as they were born.

She includes their birth announcements, a clipping of news-briefs from the day they were born, the hospital certificate, a first pair of booties, and so on for each child.

And she has them all displayed side by side on the stairway of her home, where they have become a kind of ongoing family history that everyone who visits enjoys.

So in addition to photos or pictures of some kind, you might want to have your mom or a good friend save the newspaper clippings of your engagement, wedding, and any social events that surround your wedding for such a collection. Other nice trinkets to include are a scrap of lace from your gown, the penny from your shoe, your garter, and the ticket stubs from your honeymoon trip.

These things don't add a dime to the cost of your wedding photo display, but they will add measurably to your enjoyment of it over the years.

It is also fun to include a baby picture of you and your husband if you plan to do as my friend did so the children to come can compare, as they are growing up.

Finally, if you choose a professional photographer, you'll get lots of pictures that you won't want to include in your formal collection. But most of these are just as meaningful as those "perfect" few. So don't cast them aside. Consider instead a separate album or scrapbook for these "out-takes" from your big day, and emulate a friend of mine whose sterling sense of humor gave birth to a fantastic idea.

She bought an inexpensive scrap book at the dime store and with colorful felt pens decorated the cover with the words "Our

Wedding: The Untold Story." Inside she pasted the worst of her wedding pictures, each cleverly captioned.

A photo of her father with his eyes crossed says, "Dad upon getting the caterer's bill." Another, of her mother with her hat askew, reads "Mom after the Mumms!"

I don't have to tell you that this is the album most often trotted out when company comes to call.

So have a ball at your wedding and capture it all one way or another. And whether your photos are fancy or simply snaps, perfect or far from it, you'll enjoy them for years to come, and whatever you pay for them is a good investment.

11
shower power

Nothing helps put a new household on its feet like a bridal shower.

Shower power can outfit the kitchen, linen closet, pantry or powder room. Likewise, it can add to the excitement and subtract from the work of your wedding with just a little help and creative thought on the part of your hostess—and a healthy hint or two from you.

Almost every bride these days is feted with at least one shower of some sort. There are personal showers, those of the miscellaneous variety, and specialty showers where guests are told in advance what type of gifts to bring—housewares, linens, lingerie and the like. And though the windfall of gifts is helpful to most young brides, the showers themselves are generally dull excuses for social events dreaded by most who are invited to attend them.

No matter how much the guests think of you, there is really not much about the average bridal shower to inspire excitement. Busy people would often much rather send a gift and a polite excuse for their absence than spend an entire evening playing parlor games of ancient vintage or lunching on creamed chicken, ice cream, and cake when they've been dieting.

Just as wedding trends are changing, a change in bridal showers is due. And with the current enthusiasm for nostalgia, what could be better than turning the clock back to the time when bridal

SHOWER POWER

showers were more often showers of love than showers of department store specials.

A Giant Step Backwards

In the days when bridal showers were to brides what barn raisings were to new homesteaders, the prenuptial parties were a source of excitement and delight to all invited. They were occasions when veteran homemakers had an opportunity to show off their household skills by doing some handiwork for the bride-to-be or bringing her a bounty of the best recipes their kitchens had to offer.

Those were the days when neighbors would work together in secret for weeks on a honeymoon quilt with an intricate wedding ring design, to present proudly to a young bride with their good wishes for a happy marriage sewn inside. Those, indeed, were the days!

No one has the time, and few have the talents, to duplicate such showers today, but the idea is still valid. Why not revive showers that are exciting, inspiring, and fun?

And why not let these new old-fashioned showers do double duty at the same time? How? The possibilities are endless.

First, forget the overdone showers like those for lingerie, kitchenware, and linens. These showers are so routine that they do little to encourage attendance, and so uninspiring that the guest of honor often receives doubles, triples, and quadruples of the same gifts, making them both embarrassing to the hostess and awkward for the guests.

At a personal shower I attended recently the bride-to-be received 13 half-slips, and three of them were identical, all having come from a widely advertised clearance sale at a popular department store. If a hostess suggests such a shower—and favorite aunts or godmothers are bound to—tell her you've just heard of a marvelous new kind of shower or show her this book, making certain to circle your favorites for her consideration.

What is new? Candle, wine, and gourmet showers are all on the fun list, with show-and-tell, stereo, and sentimentality showers not far behind.

What is guaranteed to bring guests out and then send them home with a pleasant memory or a new idea or two for the next shower they hostess? Something really different, like a lend-and-loan shower, a sewing bee, recipe-and-spice shower, or a basket shower!

How can you turn any shower into an aid to your wedding preparations? By suggesting that the hostess drop the parlor games and try something that memories are really made of, like letting

CANDLE, WINE & GOURMET

the guests have a hand in one or more of the routine tasks that must be done before a wedding and are accomplished easily with a large number of willing hands. She can offer them up in the guise of games if she likes, supplying prizes for the best job or the most accomplished in a given time.

A charming shower given for my daughter last spring was highlighted by a "rice bag race," in which the 15 guests were seated around a large table laden with small net squares, short lengths of ribbon and several large bowls of uncooked rice. At the start signal each guest raced to make as many individual rice bags (see page 139 for instructions) as they could in five minutes. With thirty hands flying, amid much spilled rice and laughter, more than 100 of the pretty little parcels were completed in the allotted time. A single guest did 15 to win the prize—a rice pudding recipe and a lavishly wrapped box containing all the ingredients.

The bride got the benefit of all the nimble fingers and took home a decorated wicker basket filled with the rice bags to distribute at her wedding.

The same principle can be applied to wedding or reception decorations. Tissue paper flowers, for example, are so easy to make that almost anyone can learn in minutes, and supplies are so inexpensive that every hostess can afford a lot of them.

Cut squares of the inexpensive tissue to the desired size for the flowers you plan to use. Give each guest an ample supply of squares and stem wires or chenille pipe cleaners to use as stems. A miniworkshop given by the hostess will show guests how to fan-fold the tissue, rounding off the ends, then pinching the center tightly and wrapping a stem wire around it securely. Have guests follow along with their first bloom, step by step, so that they get the feel of it from the first fold to the finale, which is separating the individual layers of the tissue and pulling them upward toward the center until a fluffy blossom is formed.

Then, allowing as little as five minutes or as long as a half-hour for the "game," depending on how many blooms you need, have each guest make as many flowers as she can in the allotted time. A prize, perhaps a pretty artificial flower arrangement or potted plant, goes to the guest who fashions the most flowers.

With a laundry basket full of the delicate-looking white or colored tissue flowers, the bride can dream up endless arrangements that will add to the decor of her wedding or reception setting.

A creative gal I recall made replicas of her old-fashioned bridal bouquet from such flowers, twisting three or four of them together, then poking the stems through a lace paper doily, lavishing the nosegay thus created with florist ribbon.

At the church she used these instead of the traditional pew-bows, hanging them from each pew by handles created from the flexible stems. Later, at the reception, she and her husband greeted guests from beneath an arbor adorned with the same beribboned bouquets, which served as a delightful backdrop for photos, too.

Another gal, whose shower hostess helped her out by having guests fashion paper flowers, turned them into topiary balls by sticking the stems into styrofoam spheres which she suspended on ribbons throughout the reception hall, for a fanciful look.

The individual flowers can be linked together by the stems into garlands as another "game," with shower guests divided into teams to see which side can create the longest garland in a given time. The fruits of their labors can be used in myriad ways to decorate at the reception or can do bumper-to-bumper duty adorning the bride's getaway car.

It's the old quilting bee syndrome with a new twist, and the brides who are benefiting by it are almost as delighted with the results as the hostesses and shower guests are with the old-fashioned fun of it all.

Whether your shower is one of these that gently "insists" that guests participate in the wedding preparations or is just one of the now showers that offers them an opportunity to come through with a bit of the stuff memories are made of, you'll enjoy the event more and your guests will, too, if your hostess has planned it with your own wedding plans in mind.

Specialty Showers

A candle shower is the perfect prenuptial party for a girl planning the "Heavenly Wedding" (page 139), for example. What could be more delightful than having an array of candles of all kinds to choose from and having guests do the shopping for you.

You can use the candles in decorating the church, the reception, and later in your apartment or home, but you can also be certain that in the soft candle glow of your wedding each guest will be looking for the candle he or she contributed to the scene, and will be proud to find it there. The unique look of a multiplicity of candles rather than carbon copies will add much to the impact of the event, too.

If you are planning a peasant wedding, a basket shower would be a boon. Wicker baskets of all sizes and shapes from laundry-basket-size down to toothpick-container proportions can all be used to advantage at the reception, both in decorating and as service pieces.

You'll heap them with paper flowers (or wild flowers in season if you're lucky); you'll cradle candles in them, pass hors d'oeuvres in them, serve pastries in them or pour wine from them, and your shower guests will have a ball picking out unusual baskets if they are given a hint of what you will use them for.

A fortunate friend from Florida who was feted at such a shower received a pair of wicker Indian Raja chairs as gifts and used them as a focal point in the garden reception, labeling them "Mr. and Mrs." for a touch of whimsy.

Gifts of Love

A lend and loan shower is a blessing to almost any bride, and to the guests too, for it allows them to spend their cash on just one present—for your wedding—and still indulge their fondness for you in some super way.

Such a shower works this way. The hostess issues the invitation with one stipulation, nothing the guests bring you is for keeps! Other than that, the sky's the limit.

This is the sort of a shower that has a surprise in every moment, for you are likely to get "presents" that a king's ransom couldn't buy.

Everything from card tables and punch bowls to candlesticks and service carts is likely to turn up. But no one can be certain just where it will all lead. The idea is that every guest brings something she thinks you might be able to use either at the wedding or the reception.

One bubbling bride got the loan of numerous silver service trays, a party percolator, and a hundred matched cups, a sixpence for her shoe, a treasured family prayer book, a rare cameo for her something old, a folding banquet table, two dozen folding chairs, a set of luggage for her honeymoon, a pair of sterling silver candelabras, a beautiful mantilla, a handkerchief carried by brides in one family for a hundred years, and a vintage limousine complete with guest chauffeur (her uncle) to get her to the church on time and in style!

The hostess has each guest sign in with name and address and the item being loaned. Guests are also urged to mark items in an inconspicuous place with their names and addresses on a piece of masking tape.

The maid of honor and best man are put in charge of returning the items while the newlyweds are honeymooning and getting the list of items and addresses to the couple as soon as they return so that thank-you notes can be sent immediately.

A simple "what would I have done without you" is enough to say, but thank-you's are a must, and loving care in using the loaned items is essential, too!

A sentimentality shower works similarly, but here the "gifts" may either be for keeps or for loan, with the guests identifying the items with tags that say either "I'm Yours" or "Return to Sender."

The object of this shower is for each guest to share with you something that is special to them and might make either your wedding or your marriage more meaningful. The item can be as personal as the handkerchief your grandmother carried at her own wedding or as delightfully different as a door-hanger that says "Do Not Disturb!" for your honeymoon suite.

A book of sonnets, a garter, a special wine for your first dinner, a list of 15 ways to say "I'm Sorry," a pledge never to go to bed on a fight, or a recipe for romance after fifty are all among the items that might be given at a shower where sentiment-in-the-making is the only criterion.

Showers should only be given by intimate friends, and therefore you should be able to talk frankly with your hostess about incorporating ideas like these into her plans. She can save you hours of labor, and put a new dimension of stretch in your bridal budget, if she will cooperate.

One thoughtful hostess, seeing that her bride-to-be was nearly frantic trying to finish her own wedding gown with the big day drawing near, asked the young girl to bring the gown to show off to wedding guests and then made a memory for everyone present by supplying each guest with a needle and thread and giving each a turn at placing a short row of stitching along the hand-rolled hem. The four-yard "problem" was solved in no time, and each guest could smile with pride at the beautiful gown on the big day, for all had had a hand in putting it together.

Here is another idea, one that was in vogue as far back as my mother's wedding shower. Each of her guests covered a button by hand for the back of her handmade wedding gown, showing their good wishes for her with the care they took to complete the buttons perfectly. The sentiment, however, is as new as today.

And here is a helpful "game" that works on the produce-against-time theory and that even shower guests who say they are all thumbs will enjoy.

The hostess supplies several boxes of plain white book matches, the kind that come 50 to a carton at the grocery store and sell for about a penny apiece. She also provides a variety of felt pens in varied shades, giving the guests only one instruction—to personalize the matchbooks with the names of the bride and groom and the wedding date in any way they wish.

Prizes are usually given for the most decorated in a given time, for the prettiest and the most original design. The bride carries away a treasury of "originals" to send home with guests as keepsakes of her wedding day.

Another idea is a "Show and Tell" shower, which is really an evening of miniworkshops where each guest brings a favorite dish for the bride and the other guests to sample, pot luck fashion, then tells how to prepare it, presenting the recipe to the bride.

Gifts for such a shower run toward unusual gadgets or appliances, and as each is opened, the sender must either demonstrate or explain how the item is used and what she particularly finds it handy for. This kind of information is the sort most homemakers require years of trial and error to collect, but can be passed on in minutes with a "toward better housekeeping" philosophy of love and fun at a shower where everybody goes home with something new to try.

A New Way to Look at Showers

Both Ann Landers and her sister Abigail Van Buren have come out in print against wedding showers as "hold-ups and frauds" and in favor of "abolishing them forever." I take a different stand.

Shower power, if returned to its roots, can be a special force that will help send you to the altar feeling loved and adored and ease you through the difficult transition from bride to wife with the wisdom of veterans to back you up.

If you can't cook, you can bluff it if you have a treasury of your family and friends' favorite recipes tucked away thanks to a recipe and spice shower. If you're uncertain which wine to serve with beef or fish, you'll pass the test with flying colors if you're the lucky woman who was guest of honor at a wine or gourmet shower where guests each attached a note to their gift of food, or drink, telling you how to serve it best. And if you thought you'd never fight, but suddenly find yourself looking for some way to say you're sorry, you'll be ever grateful for your list of 15 tested ways to say it successfully.

So don't scorn those who think enough of you to want to throw a shower. Just give them something in return, a new old-fashioned way of making it the something really special they want it to be.

12
a bouquet
of beautiful ideas

Some weddings sparkle with spontaneity. Others, for all the time and money spent on them, are lackluster affairs that seem to have been ordered from a department store catalog and staged by a window dresser.

Here is a bouquet of beautiful ideas to give your wedding a million-dollar dazzle without raising the price tag appreciably.

Rhymes with Reason

The time spent waiting for the church to fill and the ceremony to begin can seem like an eternity to early arrivals. Even those who appear promptly at the appointed hour usually are prepared to spend a restless period waiting for the wedding march to begin.

To help your wedding guests pass the time and to thank them for attending, have a member of the wedding party greet them with "Remembrance Poems" to read before the ceremony and carry home as a souvenir, afterwards.

Such poems are written by the bride or groom and worded so as to include the wedding date, a note of appreciation to the guests, the names of the bride and groom and sometimes even the couple's first address so that guests will know where to contact them after the honeymoon.

They may be handwritten, or typed in a script, and can be reproduced quite inexpensively on white paper or parchment by a photo offset process (sometimes while you wait).

The printed sheets should be rolled into small scrolls and tied with white ribbons and placed in a wicker basket to be distributed to guests as they arrive at the church.

A Tender Touch

To give a very special touch to the ceremony, have the florist who makes the bride's bouquet arrange two detachable flowers into it, tying them with ribbons like a miniature corsage.

As you step to the alter on your father's arm, stop at your mother's pew and when the minister asks who gives you in marriage, kiss your father goodbye, detach the first flower and give it to him to give to your mother as he takes his seat.

After the ceremony, as soon as the minister introduces you as husband and wife, step to your husband's family pew, detach the second flower, and give it to his mother with a kiss.

This is guaranteed to be a tear-jerker, particularly if it comes as a surprise to both mothers and guests.

Moving Ceremonies

Another moving custom that is becoming widespread today is memorizing the wedding vows and repeating them without the assistance of the minister when the moment arrives during the ceremony.

Many faiths are in favor of this idea and allow couples who so wish to depart from the traditional words and speak freely of their love in their own words rather than reciting the ritualistic vows.

Some couples recite a favorite sonnet or a passage from Kahlil Gibran. Others simply state their love and their desire to live together forever.

If you choose to do this, however, be certain to speak clearly and loudly enough that all may hear, otherwise your guests will be

uncertain of what is taking place and will miss what can be the most meaningful part of the ceremony they came to share with you. You may want to use a microphone, particularly if your wedding is outdoors!

Bridal processions traditionally see the bridesmaids and flower girls preceding the bride and her father down the aisle, with the groom and ushers joining the ladies at the altar.

But there are many more dramatic ways of arranging the processional. Royalty, as we saw at Prince Charles' and Princess Diana's wedding, lead the procession. You may choose to do that too. And just because most weddings are performed with the minister facing the congregation and the bride and groom facing him or her—with their backs to the assembled guests—this doesn't mean it has to be that way.

My good friend Karen Holmes-Feener arranged her New Year's Eve ceremony so that she and her husband stood facing guests on the top step of the altar, flanked by their attendants on descending stairs, with the minister's back to the congregation, below them.

In such a ceremony guests may enjoy sharing the look of joy on the faces of the bride and groom and have a much better chance to hear them as they recite their vows.

This situation is not advisable for the very nervous bride, however, because not only will her guests be able to see her, but she will be able to see them as well, and bridal nerves can often cause the

most serene bride and groom to become tearful when looking their parents in the eyes.

Still, this is an extremely dramatic and romantic treatment of the ceremony and provides excellent opportunities for moving photos of the exchange of vows. And, if you're opting for a garden ceremony or a casual, outdoor wedding at home, it is a very intimate arrangement.

The ancient toast, which mingles two glasses of wine from separate vineyards (one representing the personality of the bride and the other the personality of the groom) into a single glass they share, is also a romantic touch, often suggested by my dear friend Dr. Donald L. Jolly when he performs wedding ceremonies.

Three crystal goblets are placed on the altar. The minister pours wine from a separate decanter into two of the glasses and then asks first the bride and then the groom to pour a portion from each of the filled goblets into the empty one. As they are doing this, he explains to the guests that this symbolizes the preservation of the distinct personality of the bride and groom and the commingling of those personalities into a newly formed third entity, the couple.

The bride and groom then each drink half of the new mixture, reserving their half-empty goblets on the altar to show that each will retain their own identity while enjoying a new identity as well.

This ceremony is similar to the family candle-lighting described earlier but has a slightly deeper symbolism.

Just as you will want to select music that is meaningful to both the bride and groom, readings that are included in the ceremony add a meaningful touch.

If you aren't the sort who is capable of writing something original for your wedding, consult your minister for appropriate Bible scriptures that may be read aloud by members of the wedding party during the ceremony, or ask him or her if you might include a favorite poem or passage from *The Prophet*, from *Romeo and Juliet*, or from some other literary work that is meaningful to you.

Several short readings of this nature are the perfect punctuation to what otherwise might be a routine ceremony and allow you to involve special family members or friends who are not a part of the immediate wedding party.

I attended one wedding ceremony recently where a ten-year-old niece of the groom did a magnificent job of reading a Bible verse, and another where the grandmother of the bride recited a lengthy sonnet, to soft background music, as the bride and her father stepped down the aisle.

To add even more significance to such readings, ask parents and grandparents what readings were included in their wedding ceremonies and have the minister announce that the reading is the same one spoken at a previous family wedding. This can also be done with music. Just a line of introduction informing guests that the solo is the same song sung at the wedding of the bride's or groom's parents has been known to give an entire congregation goose bumps simultaneously.

Although most wedding guests attend to hear the bride and groom say their "I do's," I have attended several weddings where the guests were asked to say "I do" too. And it was an exciting moment each time.

All couples entering into marriage need the support and love of their families and friends. So what better time to remind those who care for the couple than during the ceremony.

Ask your pastor or whoever will be performing the ceremony to end your wedding by asking all present to declare their support by answering "We do" to the question, "Do all of you assembled here today to witness this marriage promise to give this new husband and wife your love and support as they begin their marital journey?" After the guests have said "We do," have the minister present you formally to them as Mr. and Mrs. John and Ellen Doe before you leave the church.

Another way to involve the congregation in the ceremony is to have all married couples present stand at a given point during the wedding and, joining hands, renew their wedding vows.

This is usually done just after the bride and groom have recited their vows and exchanged their rings, and before they are formally introduced as husband and wife.

The bride and groom may turn to face their guests and, holding hands, watch as their parents and other married couples stand and vow their own love and fidelity to one another.

When this brief ritual is complete, the minister may say something like "gentlemen, you may all kiss your brides." It is a touching sight, and one that provides an amazing feeling of love throughout the group, whether married or single.

If you choose not to have all married couples participate in a renewal of vows, you might want to include parents or grandparents of the couple in such a ceremony, asking them to step forward to the altar at the end of the ceremony and renew their wedding vows. I attended one wedding where the bride had selected her parent's silver wedding anniversary for her wedding date and included their renewal of vows in the ceremony, then shared her reception with her parents, in honor of their twenty-fifth anniversary.

I don't think a single guest left that day without commenting on what a gracious and loving gesture that was on the part of the bride.

Drawing family and friends into the ceremony can take many other forms as well. And all of them add impact and meaning to the event.

An acquaintance of mine who had lost her father as a child was given his wedding ring by her mother as a gift at her engagement. Touched deeply by this loving gesture, the bride chose to give that ring to her husband during the wedding, and as she placed it on his finger, said "With this ring, given with love by my late father, to my mother on their wedding day, I thee wed."

I guarantee you, there wasn't a dry eye in the house after that, including the groom's!

Borrow the Words

If your own words don't come easily, but you like the idea of putting together your own wedding vows, try dividing a favorite poem, each of you reciting a stanza alternately, to express your feelings for each other.

If you don't have a favorite poem, go to the public library and check out books of verse by Elizabeth Barrett Browning and Robert Browning, Rod McKuen, Carol Poliz Shultz, Kahlil Gibran, and even Shakespeare. Or refresh your memory of the Book of Psalms in your family Bible.

Perhaps you have a favorite song that suits the purpose. There are hundreds of these. Some of my favorites that work beautifully for this purpose are "The Rose" by Amanda McBroom, "For All We Know" by Robb Wilson, Arthur James, and Fred Karin, "I Love You Today" by Steve Allen, "Love Story" by Carl Sigman and Francis Lai, "With One More Look at You" by Paul Williams and Kenny Ascher, "Speak Softly Love" (the love theme from *The Godfather*) by Nino Rota and Larry Kusik, "You Needed Me" by Randy Goodrum, "You Are the Sunshine of My Life" by Stevie Wonder, "Evergreen" by Paul Williams and Barbra Streisand, and "You Light up My Life" by Joe Brooks.

If you really want to get sentimental about it, ask your parents what songs were sung at their wedding and at their parents' weddings. You may discover some real gems this way. Songs by Harold Arlen, George Gershwin, Victor Herbert, Cole Porter, Rodgers and Hart, Harry Warren, and Sigmund Romberg may not have your toes tappin' today, but many of them had lyrics that have touched the hearts of several generations.

Songs such as Gershwin's "Embraceable You," Porter's "Night and Day," Rodgers' and Hart's "With a Song in My Heart," or Harry Warren's "I Only Have Eyes for You" were popular in our parents' and grandparents' day but still convey emotions that are suitable for wedding vows as well as for wedding music.

If you're not familiar with these lyrics, go to a major music store and thumb through the old standards until you find something you both like.

And, if you sing, you might consider singing your vows to each other. But, don't contemplate this unless you are very sure of your voices and of your nerves. Even the most professional singers get choked up with emotion from time to time, and this is bound to be an emotional experience for both of you. Still, if you can pull it off, your wedding will be remembered long after many others are forgotten.

Light a Candle

The lighting of a candle symbolizing the beginning of a new family is also a very special event taking place in more and more weddings these days.

This involves three large candles, two of a color selected by the bride (usually the same color as her attendants' gowns) and a third of equal size but of purest white.

A colored candle is placed at the family pew on each side of the center aisle, to be lighted by the usher when the mothers of the bride and groom are seated, just before the processional begins.

After the couple have recited their vows, they kiss, then step from the altar together, parting momentarily at the center aisle to light a taper from their family candle. Turning with the lighted

tapers in hand, they return to the altar where the white candle is waiting to be lighted by them together, as the person performing the marriage explains the symbolic gestures.

When the light is burning brightly, the recessional begins, and the newlyweds exit from the church.

Say a Prayer

Asking the minister or judge to offer a short prayer for the blending of the two families into one, and for greater happiness for all through the union being solemnized, is a great way for both bride and groom to get off on the right foot with in-laws, and it doesn't cost a cent.

Another great way to do it is to ask each set of parents what music was played at their wedding and to include one piece from each family in the music that precedes the selections you have chosen together.

Start a Tradition

An idea similar to the flower and candle ceremonies described here is the wedding handkerchief custom. The bride prepares two dainty handkerchiefs in advance, embroidering her name and that of her husband-to-be along with their wedding date on each.

These she carries behind her bridal bouquet to be given to each of the mothers as she steps to the altar.

Given with a kiss, it is an intimate moment in the wedding that guests will long remember—and mothers of both bride and groom can always use a hanky to dab tears away during the ceremony.

The bright girl who uses this bit of sentimentality in her wedding may just be starting a family tradition—don't you wish your grandmother had thought of it? Each successive bride can add her name and wedding date to the same hankies, and soon they will be the "something borrowed" by every bride in the clan.

Fun on Wheels

To add a touch of memorable fun to the wedding festivities, supply ushers or small brothers in at. ndance with cans of aerosol shaving cream to decorate the groom's car before it leaves the church.

The foamy shave lather can be used to write "Just Married" and other slogans on the wedding car for a fluffy "frosting on the cake" effect that creates a blizzard of bubbles as the car speeds from the church.

An added bonus is that it hoses off in a hurry later and doesn't harm the paint job a bit.

To deck the wedding party cars with dainty flower garlands at just pennies each, turn the youngsters in the family, or guests at a shower, loose with a carton of facial tissue.

By pinching the individual rectangular tissues tightly together and tying them at one edge, then fanning open the upper portion, pretty paper posies can be created in seconds with spectacular results. Tie them together in strings and give them to the best man to decorate the cars with before the wedding.

Double-Duty Decor

If your bridesmaids carry baskets of flowers, make sure to have a spot for them at the reception where they can do double duty as table decorations. The women will tire of carrying them, anyway, and guests are always eager to get a closer look at the floral pieces.

One smart bride I know had her father spray an old floor-standing hat rack white for her wedding, then turned it into a flowering tree by having her bridesmaids hang their bouquets on it at the reception. It was a charming and useful decoration that delighted her guests.

For an equally whimsical touch, decorate a dress form with net and flowers as a place to put your bouquet while you cut the cake and enjoy your bridal waltz.

When you are ready to change into travel attire, have your mother display your wedding gown on it for guests at the reception as a unique decoration after you leave. Everyone wants a close look at the bridal costume, but few are able to get their fill of the wedding fluff in the press of a fast-moving reception line.

And speaking of fast-moving reception lines—there should be no other kind! See page 158.

As guests complete their trip through the reception line, the flower girl or a bridesmaid can give them individual rice bags to tear open and shower the couple with as they leave on their honeymoon.

A yard of 72-inch wide net in white or a soft pastel will be enough to make 171 of the pocket-sized pouches, which consist of four-inch squares containing a tablespoon of rice, confined bundle fashion by tying the corners of the square together tightly with narrow ribbon.

A Heavenly Touch

What's your idea of a "heavenly wedding"? Mine is one that has the maximum of romantic impact with the minimum of expense. Here's an idea that fits the bill.

Select a wedding gown of angelic style or create your own angel's robe—heavy upholstery satin wrapped at the waistline with satin drapery cords—then dress your husband-to-be and attendants (both male and female) in borrowed choir robes of a soft hue. (Speak to your minister about it early, however, or to choir directors at the local high school or college.)

To complete the picture, choose yards and yards of nylon tulle for your veil and attach it to a halo of fresh roses and baby's breath.

Give your bridesmaids similar floral halos without the veiling and have each attendant, both ushers and bridesmaids, enter the church via the center aisle before you, carrying a single white lighted taper in clasped hands. (Be sure to use a candleholder or drip guard to protect against hot wax.)

Have them form a semicircle around the minister and the groom at the altar, with candles glowing throughout the ceremony and organ music playing softly in the background. The picture will be so perfect that wedding guests will be certain heaven couldn't be any better.

~WITH CHOIR ROBES

If your wedding is to take place in the fall, save a wedding photo everyone hasn't seen to send away and have reproduced as a very special Christmas card. In black and white these cost as little as $1.50 for 20 cards and are certain to impress your friends and relatives living too distant to attend your wedding.

A fun way to top your wedding cake is to purchase a pair of small china or plastic kewpie dolls and dress them as bride and groom. This was in vogue during the 1920's and is being revived with the current enthusiasm for bygone days.

A Touch of Whimsy

And speaking of whimsy, every wedding should have a touch of it in the same way every dish needs a pinch of salt. Try any of the following ideas for the bit of fun that will help make your wedding the

140

celebration it should be rather than the solemn ritual weddings too often are.

Instead of the traditional recessional after the service, have the organist or other instrumentalist play something like "We've Only Just Begun" or "What Are You Doing the Rest of Your Life?" then join hands and rush from the church.

Borrow a special vehicle to lead your guests from wedding to reception, or to make your getaway in from the reception. If your wedding reflects the early days of the auto, a vintage car club in your area might be willing to join in the fun by providing both auto and chauffeur for the occasion.

If you've chosen a Renaissance look, you could hire a horse and wagon, or a hansom cab if yours is a wedding with a Victorian flavor.

One bride I'll never forget was a fire chief's daughter from a small Midwestern town who took leave of her guests on a shiny red hook-and-ladder truck.

13
wedding gifts

From almost the moment you announce your engagement until the eve of your wedding, friends and family will be asking you what you need or want as a wedding gift. And it's surprising how many brides have no answer for this loving question.

If you spend a few minutes with your fiancé, your mother, and others close to you considering what you actually need and what you genuinely desire, you'll be surprised how many of your wedding wishes will come true.

Everyone wants to give the bride and groom a very special gift, but few who are invited to a wedding are in a position to know what would suit your specific needs.

So dream a little, the way you did when writing a letter to Santa as a child. One clever bride of my acquaintance got out that old standby, the Sears catalog and, starting with appliances, worked her way to xylophones, noting on a pad the items that she needed or wanted in each category—*appliances, bedding, cutlery, drapes*, and so on.

Then she made notes on her color preferences and style of decor (modern, antique, contemporary, traditional, and so on) and ran off a copy of the entire list for her mother and each of her attendants. When someone asked a member of the bridal party, she had the kind of information that was really helpful, and when the gifts were opened, the bride had very few duplicates and an assortment of beautiful gifts that were appropriate to her tastes and needs.

Traditionally, many brides register at bridal centers in their favorite department stores for china, crystal, table ware, pots and pans, appliances, and the like.

This custom is very helpful to those who will be coming to the wedding from a distance. They can be referred to the bridal registry and do their shopping in a store near them, have the gift sent from the shop's location nearest the bride's home, and still be certain they are giving something she wants and needs.

To assist you in giving the kind of information wedding guests desire, the table that follows can serve as a wish list and can be copied to give to members of the wedding party and both immediate families (the persons most asked about your heart's desire).

As gifts are received, you will want to log them in in the section provided here for that purpose, and immediately respond with a thank-you note. So that you don't forget this very important task, you will find space provided to enter the date the gift arrived and the date of your thank you.

A rapid reply to a gift is meaningful to the giver and shows your genuine appreciation. Lovely person that you are, you wouldn't want anyone to think you unappreciative, so do keep track, and when you are through, you'll have a permanent record of all your wedding treasures, one that will be a heart-warming keepsake in years to come.

Just think what fun you'll have showing it to your children or grandchildren some day.

This holds true of your wedding wish list as well. Just imagine the kinds of things your mother or grandmother wanted for her first home, and you'll see why writing down your desires will be well worth the effort, even if you don't receive all of them.

I've included a space to list some dreamy luxuries among your wishes. This may be helpful to parents, who sometimes really don't know what you'd have if you could, and it also may inspire some members of your wedding party, sorority, or other group to pool their resources to purchase something you never dreamed of receiving.

My son and his bride received a beautiful gas barbecue from the best man and ushers. It has added great joy to their California living. And a good friend of mine was treated to a horse-drawn carriage to take leave of her reception just because she dreamed out loud about such a luxury. So don't be afraid to let those who love you know what you'd really like to have.

And sometimes the best wedding gifts are those that can't be bought for any price—a copy of your parent's wedding photo, a handmade lace cover for your wedding photo album, a piece of heirloom crystal or silver from within the family, a family history, a wedding poem composed by a friend, some time in a cottage of a family friend for your honeymoon, a borrowed car to get away in. Don't hesitate to add these items to your dream list. You may be sweetly surprised at the results. And those who review your list may be touched by your thoughts of what you'd treasure.

My Wedding Wish List

Colors: My personal favorite is_____

Our apartment color scheme is_____

Powder room colors_____

Kitchen colors_____

Furniture: We will be decorating in (check one) _____ Modern,

_____ Traditional, _____ Antique, _____ Contemporary,

_____ Other_____

*My china pattern is*_____

Name of manufacturer_____

*My crystal pattern is*_____

Name of manufacturer_____

*My flatware pattern is*_____

Name of manufacturer_____

*Appliances on my most-wanted list*_____

_____

_____

_____

*Linens on my most-wanted list*_____

_____

_____

Our bed size is (check one):_____ King _____ Queen _____ Full

Our bed style is (check one):_____ Standard mattress and boxspring,

_____ Waterbed, _____ Airbed, _____ Sleeper sofa

*Decorator items on my most-wanted list*_____

_____

_____

_____

*Luxury items I'd just love to have*_____

_____

_____

_____

*Little things that will mean a lot*_____

_____

_____

_____

_____

_____

*I collect*_____

_____

*He collects*_____

_____

*Things I can never get enough of*_____

_____

_____

My taste in art runs toward (check one): _____ Graphics, _____ Oil,

_____ Paintings, _____ Water colors, _____

Other (specify)_____

_____

When I select accessories I lean toward (check one):_____ Wood,

_____ Brass, _____ Silver, _____ Chrome,

_____ Ceramics, _____ Glass, _____ Other (specify)_____

Things I still need for the wedding (toasting glasses, cake server, etc.):_____

_____

_____

Our Wedding Gifts

PRESENTER	DESCRIPTION	DATE RECEIVED	THANK-YOU DATE

Our Wedding Gifts (continued)

PRESENTER	DESCRIPTION	DATE RECEIVED	THANK-YOU DATE

14
reception? no!
party? si!

What is a wedding reception? It's a little like a family reunion, a birthday party, Valentine's Day, and Christmas all rolled into one.

It's cake and ice cream, champagne and caviar, hugs and kisses, dreams coming true and good-bye to childhood forever. But best by far, it's your production and you are the star!

Planning a reception is like putting on a play. You begin with a theme and a bare stage. You add some scenery, props, a basic plot, and a cast of characters—then you pray a lot. And finally when the one-night stand is over, you spend your honeymoon nervously waiting for the reviews.

Whether they will be raves or pans depends not nearly so much on how big the production's budget was, but on how well you staged the extravaganza.

Reception Program

When you are making your reception plans, consider the order of events you plan to incorporate, as well as the customs you may want to include.

You will undoubtedly have the traditional cake-cutting ceremony and toasts by the best man, the newlyweds' dance, and some version of rice or confetti throwing at your leave-taking.

Many couples today are borrowing ethnic customs, even from

148

other ethnic groups, in order to add to the fun and merriment of the occasion.

Among the most popular of these is the "Money Dance." Traditionally Italian, the money dance has now become commonplace at weddings of all faiths and nationalities. The dance begins with the bride and groom dancing together, and when their first dance is complete, each turns to a parent (the bride to her father and the groom to his mother) to continue the dance. As the dance progresses, the groom dances with his mother-in-law and the bride with her father-in-law, and so on until each has danced with everyone at the reception briefly. The custom is, each person who shares a dance with the bride or groom places a token cash reward for the dance into the pocket of the groom or into a small basket or drawstring bag of satin carried by the bride. It is a tip honoring the newlyweds and an opportunity for guests to show their affection for the couple.

In various versions of this dance, the money may be pinned onto the bride's gown or the groom's lapels or may be incorporated into a circle dance, like that of Greek or Jewish custom.

If you will have more than forty or fifty guests at the reception, it is also nice to have a reception "coordinator" who will help keep the events on schedule.

This can be a member of the wedding party, the best man or head usher, or it can be a member of the family. Those who hire a band may want to assign the task to the band leader.

Whoever performs the duty takes the role of a master or mistress of ceremonies, calling the attention of the guests to the opening of the buffet or serving of the dinner if a full meal is to be provided, and then announcing the various events in the order that they are listed on the program.

This is particularly important if the event is being videotaped, as it lends a note of professionalism and order to what can at times be a chaotic party.

It is also a great help if the hall where your reception is being held must be vacated at a specified time in order to meet your contract or to make room for a later reception. Guests are less apt to linger on and on if they have a printed program that alerts them to the fact that the couple plans to depart at a given time, and they know all activities are officially over then.

These little programs are particularly attractive when written out in calligraphy and hand decorated, and they can be inexpensively copied at a quick printer on white parchment or pale pastel paper to match the reception decor.

The nicest I've seen were signed by the bridal couple and included a brief "Thank you for sharing this happy time with us" at the bottom.

When dealing with large groups, remember the "KISS" method—Keep It Short and Sweet.

Often less is more! A special event or two stand out in the memory. Too many "highlights" become a blur of activity, so select only those customs that are really important or meaningful to you two.

One very special custom that has gained favor again in recent years is honoring the parents of the bride and groom at the reception. This is generally done by the newlyweds themselves.

The appropriate place for this custom is right before they begin their first dance and just after they are formally introduced to reception guests.

The groom may call the guests to attention and then turn the microphone over to the bride, who will say something like, "The love of our parents produced each of us. Our love for each other would have been impossible without the loving homes in which we grew up. We are grateful for the love they have shown us and the examples they have set for us as we begin our life together."

Then the groom may introduce both sets of parents (beginning with the parents of the bride).

This may be followed by the giving of a gift from the groom to the bride's parents and from the bride to the groom's parents, something small and sentimental, such as a locket for the mothers and a key fob for the fathers, just a remembrance of the couple's admiration for their families. Or it may simply be the occasion for a family photo before the couple has the first dance.

Sometimes this custom is followed by the joining of hands of all present and a brief prayer, or the singing of a group song, perhaps "Sunrise, Sunset" from *Fiddler on the Roof.*

This touching ceremony may also take the form of a toast. However you choose to incorporate it into your plans, you can be sure that it will be a touching memory to all those present, particularly the parents who have put so much into developing you and need to know as you leave them that you still love them, although you have found someone of your own to love.

The following work space may be helpful to you in making your reception plans, for if you fill it in completely, you will have a guide to follow that everyone involved in the reception plans can use as a handy reference throughout the event.

Reception Guide

1. Menu_____

_____

_____

2. Seating arrangement for bridal party and families_____

_____

_____

_____

_____

SKETCH OF RECEPTION AREA AND SEATING PLANS

3. Flowers and decorations _____

_____

_____

4. Music (name of band and leader) and master of ceremonies _____

_____

_____

Special songs to be included _____

_____

_____

5. Cake cutting (time and details) _____

_____

6. Cake to be served by _____

7. Guest book to be attended by _____

8. Special events of the reception _____

_____

_____

9. Departure (method and time) _____

_____

10. Transportation of gifts brought to reception by _____

_____

Destination and storage of gifts_____

_____

11. Clean-up and payment of hired help (musicians, coordinators, etc.) by_

_____

(Be sure to have checks made out in advance and in envelopes)

12. Transportation of out-of-town guests to their accommodations or connections home_____

_____

Just as there is no magic recipe for a hit Broadway show, there is no formula guaranteed to produce a successful reception, one that is enjoyed by everyone—even the person who pays the bills. Still, there are a few tips that can help you avoid disaster.

Remember Your Theme

Begin with a concept, an idea that is an extension of your wedding theme. A reception need be no more than cake, punch and a receiving line, but it can include dinner, dancing, and champagne till dawn. Whether it will be plain or fancy is your first decision.

If your budget is the barest, a simple reception in the church hall with a piece of cake, a glass of punch, and an opportunity for the guests to kiss the bride is all that is necessary. Often this is all wedding guests really want anyhow.

If, on the other hand, you have saved enough on other items in your wedding budget to splurge a little, you can offer your guests a real party.

Begin reception plans in earnest by taking inventory, pooling your resources, and mustering the troops.

And Dream On

First list those items that are absolutely essential as far as you are concerned—cake, punch, a buffet, hors d'oeuvres, or (budget permitting) a full dinner. Then dream a little, adding to the list all the little niceties you really don't think you can afford—music, dancing, lavish decorations, and maybe even live entertainment.

As you did in selecting your wedding theme, dream big. Dreams are free and once expressed sometimes find ways of coming true. If no one knows that you've always dreamed of champagne flowing from a table-top waterfall on your wedding day, how can anyone help you make it happen?

Dream out loud and on paper. Talk over your dreams with anyone who will listen and pump your fiancé for secret desires he might have that would make the reception really special to him.

One bridegroom I will never forget said of his reception (which, incidentally, had set his father-in-law back $2,000) "Oh, it was all right, I guess, but it was so white and sweet. I would have given anything for a bite of chocolate cake or a can of beer!!" And why not? Many weddings today feature groom's cakes of chocolate or some other favorite flavor, just to spoil the man a little. After all, it is his wedding day, too!

Tap Your Talent Pool

Once you have both a list of "essentials" and a list of "wouldn't it be nice if we could have's," match them against that talent inventory you made of family and friends, way back when you were selecting members of your wedding party. You may be surprised to find that there, waiting in the wings, are the very supporting players you need to make your reception a smash.

Talented cousin Tommy who couldn't afford to rent a tuxedo to be your best man (and politely refused to let you pay his way, knowing that your budget was slim too) might be willing to bring a guitar and some of his musically inclined friends along to provide live entertainment for your reception.

Sorority sister Sue keeps asking "What can I do?" You love her crab-stuffed cream puffs, so let her do what she does best and have her bake up a batch to add to the reception fare.

Your sister-in-law-to-be is an art student and a whiz with papier-maché. Maybe she could whip up a whimsical centerpiece or some unusual wedding bells to spark the decor. Better yet, maybe a table-top waterfall—it doesn't hurt to wonder out loud!

If the wedding receptions you've attended just don't turn you on and you want yours to be different, try one of these tricks.

Linger Longer

Forget the reception line and instead linger at the church long enough to let all your guests assemble in the reception room, then make a grand entrance together.

Have your father offer a toast and as the guests finish it, begin the dancing, first together, then you and your father, the groom and his mother, and down the line until you have danced with every willing fellow and he with every willing woman.

You will be tired, and your shoes will be scuffed, but everyone will be having a good time by the time you are through if you insist that each partner go directly and ask someone else to dance as he leaves you.

A friendly usher assigned to keep the champagne flowing will keep you going, too. And you don't have to have a band if another usher will tend the stereo and keep the dance music running in a continuous stream, alternating fast and slow numbers so you don't get tired too quickly.

Another good way to insure everyone having a good time is giving them something to talk about. A unique way to do it is with a piñata if your reception is to be held out-of-doors.

Piñatas, the papier-maché figures Mexican children break with bats on birthdays and at Christmas, are inexpensive and can be used as decorations, for they come in every conceivable motif. Or you can make your own by decorating a hanging flower pot with fringed tissue paper.

Suspended from a rope or wire, they offer a "game" a bride and groom can play to delight their guests and get the reception off with a bang! Instead of candy, fill the piñata you will try to hit with funny fortunes—the kind you find in fortune cookies—typed or handwritten on strips of colored paper. Then when all the guests have had a glass of punch, have them gather around and blindfold

the groom. Turn him around three times and have him swing at the piñata with a bat until it breaks and the fortunes shower down on guests.

Make certain at least one of the fortunes reads, "You will be the next bride!" and another says something like, "The caterer has selected you to pay the reception bill!" Everyone likes to share his fortune, and soon all will be talking, laughing, and having a ball, including you!

Plan a Picnic

If yours will be one of the popular semiformal or informal receptions so perfect for the charming peasant or ethnic weddings of today, surprise your guests with box lunches and individual bottles of wine rather than a mountainous buffet or sterile sit-down dinner.

Fill the boxes with fried chicken and biscuits, potato salad, and rich rum cakes to take the place of a wedding cake. Tuck in napkins with your names inscribed or decorate the boxes with your names and wedding date in hot pink letters with a felt pen.

While everyone is eating, sit down and open your presents if you want to. After all, it's your party!

Decorations

Decorations from your wedding should be made to do double duty, and a member of the wedding party should be assigned to whisk them from the church to the reception and get them into place before the guests arrive. This is easily done while guests wait and watch as your wedding portraits are taken.

If bridesmaids carry baskets of flowers, assign each a spot in the reception hall to leave hers as a decoration until the event is over. Chances are she won't want to carry it while dancing or eating, anyhow.

And while you're assigning duties for the reception, decide well in advance the "who's who" of the event. It will run much more smoothly if everyone involved knows her or his role and goes to it with gusto.

Someone to cut and serve cake, someone to mix and pour punch, a special youngster to circulate the guest book, a dear aunt and some true friends to stay behind and clean up will all add measurably to the relaxed, fun atmosphere you are trying to achieve.

Who's Who

Finding out "who's who" may mean much more than who does what, however. If, for instance, there has been a divorce in either family and there is more than the normal complement of "parents" in attendance, make certain that no one is slighted in a reception line or toast. If things look as if they might get "sticky," assign someone in advance to run interference, briefing him or her in confidence about any possible problems.

If many of the "who's" will be little people and you know it in advance, plan something special to keep them amused while the adults enjoy the party. A children's refreshment table, with popcorn, peanuts, cupcakes, and punch can do wonders to avoid whining and crying while the adults get around to finally cutting the big cake or sitting down to dinner.

Even if you are certain the majority of those attending the reception will be friends of your own generation, don't forget about the "old folks." Provide a slow dance occasionally, enough seats grouped for conversation, and pay enough attention to them to let them know you really wanted them present.

Forget the Receiving Line

A receiving line has long been the accepted way of greeting guests and giving them an opportunity to express their congratulations and best wishes. But far from being a high point of the postnuptial party, it is usually an endurance test for reception guests.

At a wedding I attended last spring it was one hour and forty minutes before the bride and groom were free of the receiving line to cut the cake and get on with the reception. Some guests, who had traveled long distances by car, had to leave before the champagne was opened, and one elderly woman became faint for waiting in the warm hallway so long to kiss and congratulate the newlyweds.

If you have ever had to stand in line for more than fifteen minutes, you know what a colossal bore it can be, and waiting for an hour can seem an eternity when the reward for your wait is simply a tired handshake and a kiss from a bride who has nearly lost her pucker! What can you do to keep your guests from feeling the same way?

You could skip the receiving line entirely. I did at my own wedding and my daughter did, too. To tell you the truth, not one guest seemed to miss it.

Many brides today are taking this way out, although I must admit that I thought it was "devilish" when I did it, years ago.

What I did, instead, was exactly what my daughter and her husband did recently, and it worked out beautifully.

First we planned a photo session at the church following the ceremony but assigned some good friends to the reception site to open the doors and get the punch bowl going. They also got music started and refreshments circulating.

Then we urged ushers to direct guests to the reception room so that the majority of our guests would be able to have a glass of champagne punch and a bite to eat while we were posing for the photographer.

Finally, we made a grand entrance together, shaking hands, kissing, and talking briefly to guests as we made our way to the refreshment table. There, my father offered a toast to our health and happiness, and the party was on its way.

After the toast, we took our place behind the wedding cake for more pictures, which ended with the cutting of the cake. And then, much to our guests' surprise, we served the cake ourselves!

As guests stepped up to the cake table, we exchanged greetings, thanked them for coming, and received their good wishes. We found that everyone took turns, coming up in a steady stream, but no one waited in line. Instead they enjoyed another drink, chatted in small groups over hors d'oeuvres, or admired the display of gifts until there was room at the refreshment table for them to step up.

Our reception was many years ago, but our daughter's last June proved that this method still works. It takes far less time to greet all your guests this way because they don't have to go through handshaking ceremonies with your entire wedding party, feeling as though they must say a few words to everyone. They know they'll get a turn to visit with you as they get their cake, and they make it brief because they know others are anxious for a taste of the wedding fare, too. Both Nancy and I found this a delightful way to dispense with the formal receiving line and get the reception off to a good start.

This method could be varied by tending the punch bowl instead, but people seem to come back to it too often. Guests seldom make the cake trip more than once.

Cutting and serving 100 pieces of cake should take less than

YOU SERVE THE CAKE !

half an hour, and once it is done you will be free to eat, dance, and mingle with your guests. While you are busy, your mother and father can introduce your in-laws to guests personally, and your bridesmaids, ushers, and other wedding party members can circulate refreshments, serve punch, and attend to music.

If you insist on a reception line, or if your mother does, make it one where guests greet only you and your spouse, at the door.

Station your parents at another point in the room (the punch bowl, perhaps), and direct guests to them, where they can chat with either couple at their leisure, or not at all if they choose. This is particularly helpful in weddings where there are multiple "parents," for it avoids the awkwardness of explaining 100 times, this is Mrs. XX, the bride's stepmother and this is Mr. ZZ, the groom's stepfather, and so on. You are the one the reception guests are really waiting to see and if they want to talk to your mother, stepfather, or Aunt Hilda, they will seek them out in the crowd.

15

reception recipes
that cater to you

Even if you've never given a party for more than ten people in your life, you can cater your own wedding and do it beautifully, with just a little help from your friends.

Do you think the caterer does all the cooking? Of course not. The caterer plans the menu, selects time-tested recipes, and then puts a crew to work on them, preparing as many as possible well in advance of the big day. You can do the same.

Wedding food is like no other. It must be lovely to look at, delightful to eat, and easy to fix. And if you are planning to prepare it in advance, it must feature recipes that freeze or store well.

In planning a reception menu you should consider the fact that unless you have table seating for as many guests as you expect, the majority will be eating your wedding fare with a plate balanced on one knee, a drink in one hand, and nothing more than a fork to attack it with.

Feature Finger and Fork Foods

With that in mind, I have selected a variety of hot and cold dishes, appetizers, and sweets that either can be eaten properly with the fingers or are easy to manage with just a fork. Without table space for each guest, foods that require a knife are definitely out. Likewise, spoon foods that are liquid or slippery (soups or gelatins) are quite hard to handle when diners are moving about and the room is crowded. Tomato aspic on Aunt Tillie's new gown can end a beautiful reception on a sour note.

No collection of reception fare would be complete without punch recipes, so we have included a bowlful of recipes for group grog that is bound to please.

So easy, good, and inexpensive are these recipes that I'll bet you'll be using them for entertaining for years to come.

NEVER-SOGGY APPETIZERS

1. Prepare your favorite smooth sandwich spread. If the recipe doesn't include cream cheese, add it and increase the seasoning, adding food coloring, too, if you desire.

2. Place a piece of waxed paper on a cookie sheet and trace designs from a cookie cutter onto it—hearts, diamonds, spades and so forth.

3. Fill a cookie press with the sandwich spread and press onto the waxed paper, filling in the outlines you have made.

4. Quick-freeze these, then peel off the waxed paper and store the motifs in a freezer bag until your wedding day.

5. Cut white, wheat, rye, and pumpernickel bread shapes with the same cookie cutters you used as patterns, and freeze.

6. The day of the wedding, pop the frozen sandwich-spread motifs onto the matching bread pieces and arrange on trays covered with lace paper doilies. Garnish with pimiento, olive slice, or pickle spear for added color, and trim each tray with a wreath of parsley for a professional touch.

SHRIMP BALLS

If you love shrimp but can't afford huge bowls of it to serve at your reception, consider stretching what you can afford with this recipe.

3 cups cooked shrimp, chopped
1½ cups shredded wheat wafer crumbs
½ teaspoon salt
¼ teaspoon pepper
3 eggs

1 clove garlic, minced
1/2 cup melted butter
Mix shrimp, wafer crumbs, salt, pepper, and eggs and let stand for ten minutes. Melt butter in medium frying pan on medium heat and add minced garlic.

Shape shrimp mixture into small balls about one inch in diameter. Sauté shrimp balls in butter until golden brown all around. Serve hot with tartar or shrimp sauce. Yield: 36.

SEAFOOD COCKTAIL SAUCE

1/2 cup catsup
1/4 cup chili sauce
1 1/2 teaspoons horseradish
1/2 teaspoon Worcestershire sauce
1/2 lemon, cut in pieces
Place all ingredients in blender at low speed until smooth, for one cup of sauce. Serve with shrimp balls, shrimp, lobster, crab, or oysters as budget permits.

JIFFY SWEET AND SOUR SAUCE

Your guests will know you're a secret gourmet when you serve this surprisingly simple sweet and sour sauce over your favorite meatballs or sliced frankfurters.

Combine one ten-ounce jar of grape jelly and one twelve-ounce bottle of chili sauce in a skillet and stir on low heat until mixed and smooth. Add meatballs or franks and continue to cook slowly for half an hour. Meatballs are not browned first, so this is a one-pan dish and if you're smart, you'll select an electric skillet or fondue pot that goes directly on the buffet table to keep the contents warm throughout the event.

SPACE-AGE STROGANOFF

This elegant basis for an unforgettable wedding dinner can be completed in 15 minutes and will have your guests certain someone was slaving over it for hours.

For each six servings you will need:

1 pound round steak
3 tablespoons butter
2/3 cup water
1 three-ounce can broiled, sliced mushrooms
1 envelope onion soup mix
1 cup dairy sour cream
2 tablespoons enriched flour
buttered fine noodles or rice

Trim fat from meat and cut diagonal strips across the grain ¼ inch wide. Heat butter in skillet, then brown meat quickly on medium heat. Add water, mushrooms (including liquid), and soup mix and heat on high just until boiling.

Blend in sour cream and flour then cook and stir on low heat until mixture thickens. Sauce will be thin. Serve over hot noodles.

MAGNIFICENT MUSHROOMS

This recipe is so simple you'll be surprised you haven't thought of it yourself.

For fabulous marinated mushrooms select fresh mushrooms from the market, a day or two before you plan to serve them. At the same time buy one 8-ounce bottle of Italian salad dressing for each half-pound of mushrooms purchased.

Thoroughly wash mushrooms and place in plastic container with tight-fitting lid. Pour the Italian dressing over the mushrooms and allow to stand overnight. Serve with dressing in a pretty glass dish, garnishing with parsley flakes and providing party picks for spearing.

CHEESE BALL SUPREME

1 large package Philadelphia cream cheese
1 small jar Old English cheese spread
4 ounces Roquefort cheese
pinch of salt
1/2 pound pecans

1 small onion
1 clove garlic
½ bunch parsley

Mix cheeses together. Put pecans, onion, garlic, and parsley through grinder individually or chop finely. Then add onion, garlic, salt, and half of nuts and half of parsley. Shape into a ball, then roll in remaining nuts and parsley.

Arrange in center of large plate and surround with several kinds of crackers.

INDIVIDUAL DATE CAKES

1⅔ cups flour
3 teaspoons baking powder
½ teaspoon cinnamon
½ teaspoon nutmeg
½ cup soft unsalted sweet butter
1⅓ cups brown sugar, firmly packed
2 eggs
½ cup milk
½ pound dates, finely chopped

In a large bowl sift together flour, baking powder, and spices. Add remaining ingredients, except for dates, and beat at medium speed for three minutes.

Mix in dates by hand, then spoon into greased and floured muffin tins and bake at 350 degrees for 40 minutes or until a toothpick comes out clean when inserted in the center of the cake. Top individual cakes with butter cream frosting roses or other decorations if desired. Display in fluted paper muffin cups of pastel shades. Yield: 8.

INDIVIDUAL FRUIT CAKES

1 cup candied fruits, chopped
1 cup walnuts, chopped
5 tablespoons Triple Sec Liqueur
1¼ cups butter
½ cup granulated sugar
½ cup honey
1 tablespoon orange peel, grated
4 eggs, separated

2 cups flour
1½ teaspoons baking powder
Combine fruit, nuts and liqueur and let stand. Cream together butter and sugar, add honey and orange peel, and continue beating until fluffy. Add egg yolks one at a time, beating after each addition. Combine flour and baking powder, sprinkling half a cup of the mixture over fruit and nuts. Add floured fruit with remaining flour to batter and stir well but do not beat. Whip egg whites until stiff but not dry, then fold into cake batter.

Pour into well-greased muffin tins (or tins lined with paper cupcake liners) and bake in moderate oven at 350 degrees for 40 minutes or until toothpick inserted in the center comes out clean.

Cool thoroughly then wrap and freeze. Thaw at room temperature to serve, and for a nice touch, glaze with a very thin confectioners' sugar icing (mix confectioners' sugar and water) just before serving. Yield: 15.

NEVER-FAIL FRIED CHICKEN

For each chicken have ready:

½ cup flour
1½ teaspoons salt
1½ teaspoons paprika
enough salad oil for frying
Combine flour, salt, and paprika and roll chicken pieces in the mixture.

Pour enough oil into a large skillet to cover the bottom. Heat and fry the chicken in the hot oil, turning to brown evenly. Cover and cook slowly 20 to 25 minutes.

To freeze, cool chicken thoroughly, then place chicken pieces on a baking sheet and freeze until firm. Remove from freezer long enough to wrap pieces individually in moisture-proof wrap, pressing the material against the chicken firmly to press out as much air as possible.

To serve, remove wrap. Heat 1 or 2 tablespoons butter and 1 or 2 tablespoons of water in a heavy skillet. Place chicken in skillet, cover tightly, and turn heat to low. Let thaw slowly until piping hot, about 15 minutes.

SESAME CAKES

For each two dozen of these tasty, tiny cakes have ready:

2 cups of flour
1½ teaspoons baking powder
½ cup sugar
¼ teaspoon salt
½ cup lard
¼ cup cold water
2 egg whites
sesame seeds

Sift the flour, baking powder, sugar, and salt together. Blend in the lard, then add water to make a soft dough.

Shape the dough on a floured board into a roll about 1½ inches thick and roll it in wax paper. Chill it for two hours or more.

Cut the chilled dough into ¼-inch rounds. Coat them lightly with egg whites and press the coated side into a mound of sesame seeds.

Place the cakes on an ungreased baking sheet in the oven at 350 degrees for 20 minutes until brown. Yield: 2 dozen.

CHICKEN CHOW MEIN (Soft)

For each six guests you plan to serve prepare:

1 pound noodles
¼ pound white cabbage, onions, celery or bean sprouts
a few Chinese dried mushrooms, bamboo shoots, or fresh mushrooms
¼ pound cooked chicken
4 ounces lard
2 tablespoons soy sauce

Boil the noodles for five minutes in plenty of water. (When they float they will be ready.) Then drain and spread them out flat on a plate or platter.

Cut vegetables and cooked chicken into thin strips and fry in one ounce of hot lard for five minutes; add one tablespoon soy sauce and mix well.

Fry the noodles separately in lard for five minutes and add remaining tablespoon of soy sauce. Combine all ingredients and fry for another five minutes.

TAMALE PIE

Hot and hearty, this is a penny-wise dish with a zesty flavor certain to be a hit with guests of all ages.

For every six guests you will be entertaining, fix:

2 cups cornmeal
1½ teaspoons salt
6 cups boiling water
1 pound ground beef
1 medium onion, chopped
2 cups tomatoes
salt and pepper to taste
2 tablespoons chili powder
1 medium can black olives

Combine cornmeal with salt in boiling water until it forms mush, then set aside.

Cook beef and onion until brown. Then add tomatoes, salt, pepper, and chili powder and boil gently until slightly thickened.

Line baking dish with mush on bottom and sides, then pour in meat mixture and dot top with more mush. Bake at 350 degrees for 30 minutes. Garnish with the olives.

GUACAMOLE

A great dip for chips or strips, guacamole is a favorite in Southern California and throughout the Southwest.

To make a large bowlful you will need:

2 medium tomatoes, peeled and chopped
2 tablespoons onion, minced
1 teaspoon chopped green chilis
2 tablespoons vinegar
1 teaspoon salt
¼ teaspoon freshly ground pepper
2 mashed avocados

Combine tomatoes, onion, chilis, vinegar, salt and pepper. Let stand one hour, then add avocados, blending until smooth. Do not prepare too far in advance, as the mixture will darken with exposure to air. If you must store for more than an hour or two, keep in tightly sealed (airtight if possible) plastic container.

WATER CHESTNUT RUMAKI

An ideal appetizer to make and freeze ahead in quantity, this treat is at home on an authentic Japanese menu.

12 chicken livers
36 water chestnuts
9 slices bacon
1/2 cup soy sauce
1/8 teaspoon powdered ginger
    Cut livers into three pieces each and fold around water chestnuts. Wrap a piece of bacon around the liver and fasten with a toothpick. Blend soy sauce and ginger in bowl and marinate pieces for one hour. Drain and place on rack in shallow pan, then bake at 450 degrees for 15 minutes or until bacon is crisp. Yield: 36.

STUFFED MUSHROOMS

These are so good you can bet nobody will eat just one, so better prepare in quantity.

24 mushrooms caps, medium in size
2 tablespoons butter
2 tablespoons green onion, chopped
2 cans liver paté
1 1/2 teaspoons vinegar
1 teaspoon curry powder
2 1/2 teaspoons Worcestershire sauce
chopped parsley
grated Parmesan cheese
    Remove stems from mushrooms and chop fairly fine. Melt butter and sauté chopped stems and onion until limp. Add liver paté, vinegar, curry, parsley, and Worcestershire sauce. Stuff this mixture into mushroom caps and place on a flat pan; sprinkle with Parmesan cheese; then bake for 15 minutes at 450 degrees. Yield: 24.

MEXICAN WEDDING CAKES

Light and just barely sweet, these individual cakes are the kind enjoyed at Mexican peasant weddings for centuries. And, if they cost any less to make they'd be free!

To make five dozen have ready:

1 cup soft butter
½ cup confectioners' sugar, sifted
2 cups all purpose flour
¼ teaspoon salt
1 teaspoon vanilla extract
Cream butter and ½ cup confectioners' sugar until fluffy. Add remaining ingredients and mix well.

Pinch off small pieces of the dough and shape into finger-size logs. Place on an ungreased cookie sheet and bake about 10 minutes at 375 degrees. While hot from the oven, roll in unsifted confectioners' sugar.

These may be kept fresh in an airtight container or frozen until needed. Yield: 5 dozen.

CANDIED NUTMEATS

1 cup sugar
½ teaspoon cinnamon
½ teaspoon ginger
¼ teaspoon nutmeg
¼ teaspoon cloves
¼ teaspoon cream of tartar
½ cup boiling water
3 cups fancy mixed nutmeats
1 teaspoon pure vanilla extract
Combine sugar, spices, cream of tartar, and water in saucepan and bring the syrup to a boil. Cook to the firm ball stage, or 250 degrees on a candy thermometer. Remove from heat and stir in the nutmeats and vanilla. Continue mixing gently until the sugar crystallizes.

Turn onto a marble slab or two layers of heavy waxed paper, separating the nuts slightly. Allow them to cool and dry completely before storing them in airtight jars.

CHEESE GRITS

1 cup grits
4 cups boiling water
3 eggs, separated
3 tablespoons butter
3 tablespoons flour
1½ cups milk
½ cup Old English cheese, grated

Boil grits in the 4 cups of water until thick. Then cool one hour, stirring occasionally. While hot, add three small egg yolks, one at a time, and beat after each addition.

Prepare a white sauce of the butter, flour, and milk. Cook until thick and add cheese. Fold in stiffly beaten egg whites, then pour into baking dish, covering the mixture with cheese on top. Bake 45 minutes at 350 degrees. Serves six.

HOT CHEESE SURPRISES

½ cup butter
2 cups shredded cheddar cheese
1 cup sifted flour
½ teaspoon salt
⅛ teaspoon cayenne

Cream butter and cheese. Sift flour, salt, and cayenne and mix well with cheese. Shape into one-inch balls and stuff each with a green olive or cocktail onion.

Freeze until ready to cook, then bake at 350 degrees for 15 minutes or until puffed and lightly brown. Makes about 40 puffs.

Special Sandwich Spreads
To Freeze Ahead

EGG

Sieve six large egg yolks (hard-cooked), add ½ cup soft margarine, ½ cup finely chopped ripe olives, 2 tablespoons prepared mustard, ¼ teaspoon salt, ¼ teaspoon onion powder and

¼ teaspoon tabasco sauce. Blend thoroughly. Makes about three cups or enough for four dozen canapes.

CRAB

Combine one 7-ounce can of crab meat with 3 tablespoons of salad dressing, 2 tablespoons of catsup, 1 tablespoon lemon juice, ½ teaspoon pepper. Blend thoroughly. Makes about two cups or enough for three dozen canapes.

HAM

Combine 2 cups ground cooked ham with ¼ cup minced parsley, 2 tablespoons dairy sour cream, and 2 tablespoons horseradish. Blend thoroughly for enough spread to create about four dozen canapes—approximately 2½ cups.

CHEDDAR

To 2 cups shredded cheddar cheese add ⅓ cup light cream, 3 tablespoons minced onion or chives, 1 tablespoon catsup, 1½ teaspoons Worcestershire, ¼ teaspoon salt and a dash of cayenne. Blend well, then beat until fluffy. Makes about 2 cups or enough to spread 32 canapes.

When preparing canapes for the freezer, spread the bread with a thin layer of butter to keep it from becoming soggy. Top the butter with the desired spread and add any garnishes except fresh vegetables like parsley or tomato, (They will wilt.) Wrap completed canapes well and freeze. To serve, remove approximately half an hour before reception or just before leaving for the church. Uncover when you return.

Punch for the Bunch

Though many well-heeled brides plan an open bar or purchase champagne by the carload to insure sparkling postnuptial parties,

4

if you are hoping to keep reception costs under four figures, punch for the bunch is your best bet. With a punch bowl you control both the amount of alcohol consumed and the kind and cost of mixes used.

There are as many kinds of punches as there are people, and everyone has a favorite, whether strictly nonalcoholic or provocatively potent. Here are a half-dozen recipes which run the gamut. One is bound to be just what the parson ordered—probably the first one.

MOCK CHAMPAGNE

This one's a fooler! Not a drop of the bubbly but a zesty good taste that's certain to make Aunt Minnie wonder if she's tipsy after her third cup.

For each ten servings combine one cup sugar and one cup water and boil five minutes. Add one cup unsweetened grapefruit juice and a half-cup orange juice. To this add $\frac{1}{3}$ cup grenadine syrup, then chill.

This is your punch base. Just before serving add two 7-ounce bottles of cold ginger ale. Serve in champagne glasses, and when you taste it you'll wonder yourself if someone spiked it.

ROSÉ PUNCH

Inexpensive and easy, this pretty pink punch is light enough to be enjoyed in quantity without worry about tipsy guests. It's tangy enough, however, to satisfy like champagne.

Begin by placing an ice ring in a large punch bowl. (To make an ice ring, pour water into any ring mold and freeze.) Add $\frac{1}{2}$ gallon of chilled rosé wine, one tall bottle of ginger ale, a like amount of vodka mixer, and a 6-ounce can of orange juice. This will be enough for about 30 servings.

To stretch the recipe and add an extra punch (you little devil, you) pour in a fifth of vodka when no one is looking!

PRIM'S CHAMPAGNE PUNCH

Better tasting than straight champagne and one-fourth as expensive, this delightfully simple recipe is a simple delight. Brought from Australia by a family friend, it was the recipe selected by my daughter for her wedding.

Combine equal parts of chilled champagne, pineapple juice, chablis wine, and ginger ale. Garnish with fresh strawberries or serve with a red, ripe strawberry in each champagne glass or punch cup.

RUM AND BRANDY SURPRISE

Caution! Tasting too frequently before the wedding may cause you to forget the whole thing.

Begin by placing ¾ cup of fine granulated sugar and 1 quart lemon juice in a large punch bowl. Stir until sugar is dissolved. Add 2 quarts light rum, 1 quart brandy, 2 quarts water, and 3½ ounces of peach brandy, in that order. Allow to "marry" for at least two hours, stirring occasionally. The results are spectacular! A little really goes a long way.

EXPORT

It gets its name from the fact that you can suddenly find yourself checking out if you drink too much of this punch. It's easy to make by the gallon for a crowd, even for novice "bartenders."

Combine equal parts of grapefruit juice, rum and sweet vermouth. Pour over ice and garnish with mint leaves.

CHATHAM ARTILLERY PUNCH

Serve this one with a 21-gun salute, for your guests will still be getting a kick out of it in the morning. A really wild way to start a honeymoon!

174

This one takes two days to prepare but is well worth it if your friends are the kind who demand a real sock in the punch.

For the punch base prepare a large container with 2 gallons of Catawba wine, 1½ quarts of gin, 1 gallon Puerto Rican rum, 1 quart brandy, 1 pint Benedictine, 2 quarts rye whiskey, 2 gallons tea, 2½ pounds brown sugar, the juice of a dozen oranges and a dozen lemons, and 2 quarts vodka—steep for 48 hours before your wedding day.

Make up several large cakes of ice—pretty, heart-shaped molds do wonders for making this punch look demure—and place one in the punch bowl each time you fill it.

Pour over the ice five bottles of champagne, then fill the bowl to the brim with the punch base and stir gingerly.

Serve in small cups and instruct guests to drink with caution. The taste will be somewhat like sparkling iced tea, but every cupful packs a wallop that won't be forgotten for weeks.

It's a real winner, however, if there's even the slightest hostility between the clans. Two cups of this and everyone is just one big, happy family.

BORDER BUTTERMILK

White and frothy, like an innocent dairy drink, but with a kick that makes you shout "olé."

Combine equal parts of frozen lemonade, tequila and ice in a blender. Let spin half a minute until foamy and then serve.

Be Creative with the Cake

Of all the reception fare, the cake is just about the only mandatory item. Today, wedding cakes are taking on new dimensions in keeping with the varied "do your own thing" weddings of the times.

Tricia Nixon's famed tower of lemon cake and icing may have been supremely suitable to a White House wedding, but if you are cost conscious, forget the culinary nightmares such cakes involve.

Better to select a time-honored recipe and a simple design, using ingenuity rather than hours of labor to produce a striking effect.

Stack It

One of the prettiest wedding cakes I've seen was created pyramid fashion from three sheet cakes simply decorated with roses and icing swags. Two of the identical cakes were set side by side, leaving a space of about three inches between them. In the center of each cake were two inverted champagne glasses with sugar doves and a single rose trapped inside. The third cake was placed atop the inverted goblets like a bridge between the two lower cakes. At one corner of the top cake were two more champagne glasses, this time upright, each with a sugar dove fixed to the rim with frosting. The doves held streamers that came together in a bow, linking a pair of outsized wedding rings at the opposite corner of the cake.

Link It

Similar things can be done with sheet cakes of varying sizes. A talented friend once made a marvelous cake for a small wedding by cutting hearts from two large sheet cakes, decorating them lavishly, and linking them with a sugar bridge purchased from a bakery supply house.

A small bride and groom were placed on the bridge, and the entire cake was placed on a rectangular mirror where blown-glass swans, their hollow backs filled with fresh flowers, made a charming picture.

The cost of the entire setting, with ample cake for 50 guests, was under $15.00.

If you have no baking or decorating talents in the family, consider purchasing a small commercial wedding cake and augmenting it for pennies with gaily decorated pastries by using this trick:

Buy packages of prepared lunch-box cakes—Twinkies, Zingers, Googles, and the like. They come two or three to a package at the corner grocery store and cost very little. There are several varieties—sponge or chocolate cake with assorted fillings and toppings, some frosted and others plain.

First freeze them, then cut off the ends diagonally, exposing the cream centers. If they are unfrosted, spread a thin layer of butter cream frosting over the tops and decorate with silver dragees, a small rose, or other frosting motif. Arrange them in fluted pastry papers, then pop them back in the freezer until it is time to serve them.

Flank or Ring It

At the reception, display these individual wedding pastries on silver cake plates flanking the main cake. They will add a note of color and elegance to the table and make perfect "carry home to sleep on cakes" for the unmarried women in the crowds.

No one will ever guess that they didn't come from the smartest bakery in town if you don't get so excited about the way they look and taste that you spill the beans. An added bonus is that these tasty treats are just as delicious directly from the freezer as they are thawed.

If you warn guests in advance (so that nobody breaks his or her bridgework), you can slip a shiny new penny inside one of the small cakes to determine who will be the next one married. This is an ancient European custom that is certain to delight the single women in attendance and cause untold pain to their dates. But, it's all in the name of fun.

Another great way to use the individual cakes is to build a latticework "wall" around the base of your wedding cake with them, elevating the main cake on a footed plate to give it more stature, then surrounding it with the small cakes piled neatly, two or three high.

Build Your Own

If you are daring, you might consider carrying this trick a step further by forgetting the bakery wedding cake altogether and "building" your own easy-serve cake, building-block style, from the Twinkie or Zinger style cakes that come two or three to a package at the grocery store.

Buy the unfrosted kind (at three to a package you can get 100 for $16) and frost them yourself in white buttercream icing. Then on a large cake plate, or covered cardboard base, stack them as you

" TWINKIE TOWER "

would blocks (leaving a space in between like a window) until you have the effect you like best—a lacy pyramid, a clever castle, an ivory tower, or whatever strikes your fancy.

Work quickly, using additional frosting for "mortar" as you go. When you are through, place a sugar dove, frosting rose, bell, or other motif in each of the windows and add a bride and groom at an appropriate spot.

When it comes time to serve the cake, you have it made, for each "building block" is an individual serving, and all you have to do is lift them easily with a server and they will separate without spilling a crumb.

The bride who showed me this neat trick had selected a Camelot theme for her large wedding. Using 200 of the lunch-box cakes, she created a shimmering castle, aglow with silver dragees and sugar bells and complete with bride and groom standing on a sugar drawbridge in front.

Guests were amazed at the fanciful castle, and not one guessed the secret even after they had eaten the cream-filled sponge cakes used to build it.

A Pair Extraordinaire

If your reception will be just family and close friends and you don't want to go to all the trouble and expense of a formal wedding cake, have your mother make a "Groom's Top Hat" and a "Bride's Bouquet" cake to add a note of whimsy to the event.

For the groom's cake, stack five eight-inch chocolate layers atop a 12-inch cardboard circle, spreading each layer with rich, dark chocolate frosting.

Then frost top and sides of the tall cake smoothly, bringing frosting down to cover the cardboard base, too. When that is done, create a hatband around the base with milk chocolate frosting, or a soft, contrasting color.

To create the bride's bouquet, you will need a dozen sugar ice-cream cones (the pointed kind), a dozen white cupcakes, butter frosting in several pastel shades, a pretty wicker basket lined with lace paper doilies, and a spool of florist ribbon and tape.

Begin by placing the small end of each cupcake into the open end of each ice-cream cone as if it were a large flower. Using a pastry tube and varied tips, you will find that you can easily create fluffy mums, darling daisies, and full-blown roses if you work at it.

Add frosting leaves around the base of each flower, then arrange them in the basket as you would if they were real flowers. Finally, fill in the spaces with small bows of white satin florist ribbon, and add a bow and some streamers at one side.

Wedding Book Place two sheet cakes side by side and frost as one, decorating as if it were an open book. Inscribe it "Our Wedding" and include the date and your names, if you like.

His and Hers

A pair of 12-inch round layers and a single nine-inch square cake are the components of one of the cutest 'his and hers' cakes ever.

Decorated to resemble a bride and groom cheek-to-cheek, this clever cake is easy enough for even a beginner to create at home.

Begin by preparing a piece of masonite or heavy cardboard 15″ × 30″ by covering it with paper and lace doilies.

Gather a piece of white net, 12″ × 24″ size, about four inches down from the long edge. Then staple the "veil" thus formed to the base, six inches to the right of center and about four inches down from the top, placing the staples along the gathering line.

Frost the two round cakes in a pale pink shade (or whatever

flesh color desired) and place them on the prepared base so that the center edges are touching and one cake is positioned upon the netting to look as if it is wearing a veil.

From the square cake cut a rectangle three inches high by two inches wide, and a strip one inch wide and three inches long. These form the top hat for the groom and should be frosted in chocolate, then placed atop the groom's cake at a jaunty angle. A bow tie is formed by cutting two equilateral triangles from the square cake, two inches on a side. Frost them in chocolate and place them under the "chin" of the groom's cake.

A crown, three inches wide and two inches tall, should be cut from what remains of the square, frosted in white, and placed atop the bride's cake head.

With this basic work done, use a toothpick to draw a face and hair on each cake in cartoon fashion. You can draw and erase as much as you like by simply smoothing the icing with a knife until you get the faces you like best. Or you can copy the illustrations shown here.

Once you have the outlines, use a finetipped pastry tube to "color them in." Complete the enchanting picture by lavishing the bride's crown with flowers (if you're not good at making them yourself, they can be purchased frozen from a cake decorating shop) and a row of ruffled icing under her chin.

Be a Friend of the Baker

If your budget doesn't demand a do-it-yourself cake but you want to use one of these ideas, anyway, have a heart-to-heart talk with your local baker. Tell him or her you want something really different and explain how you can have it by using one of these easy-to-put-together methods. Stress that although perhaps the baker never made such a cake before, you are giving him or her free an idea that could bring untold profits in the future.

If you're as sweet as sugar and frosting on a cake, the baker just might come through with a special discount for your "brilliance" or agree to throw in the bride and groom figures at no extra charge.

Topping It Off

And speaking of the cute couple that will top your cake, they can be outrageously expensive. If you would rather see that money spent elsewhere—on your honeymoon souvenirs, maybe—try one of these tricks for creating your own cake top.

1. From the florist supply house nearest you, purchase a pair of white feather doves. Place in their beaks dime-store diamond rings linked with satin streamers. Then arrange the birds atop a styrofoam pedestal, using pearl-headed pins to fasten them securely.

For a delicate look, trim the base with lace paper doily motifs secured with more pearl-topped pins.

2. A large pair of sugar bells from the bakery supply store placed in front of a small paper fan from the ten-cent store makes a sentimental-looking top for any wedding cake. These can be set right into the top layer of the cake with frosting or mounted on a styrofoam round of appropriate size.

If the latter is done, frost the foam base to look like an additional layer on the cake.

3. Build a sugar cube church to top your cake and set it in a garden of fresh flowers on your wedding day.

To build the church, cut a block of styrofoam three inches by four inches and two pentangular end pieces three inches square. Attach the two end pieces to the block with frosting, then working rapidly, "cement" the sugar cubes to the church base with more frosting.

When all sides are covered, cut a rectangle of heavy construction paper 4″ × 6″ for the roof and attach it to the styrofoam with pins. Use thin mints or similar white candies for shingles, affixing them with additional icing.

To form a bell tower or steeple, build a stack of sugar cubes up one side of the church (attaching with icing) and pitch a tiny roof atop it as you did on the main building. Then finish it off with a sugar bell.

You can trim the chapel in myriad ways, using candies or ic-

182

ing. When the big day comes, place it atop your cake and surround it with fresh flowers.

4. Build a tiny trellis from chenille stems (we always called them pipe cleaners) and cover it with lace. Center it in a styrofoam round, three inches in diameter, then lavish the base with lace ruffling, held in place by pearl-headed pins poked through the center of iridescent sequins.

Suspend a dainty plastic or sugar bell (no larger than one inch in size) from the top and stand a tiny bride and groom beneath it.

5. For a Valentine's Day wedding, fashion a heart about five inches high from chenille stems and fasten it to a styrofoam round three inches across.

Fold a rectangle of net five by ten inches into accordian pleats and press them in place. Staple the folded net at the base, then unfold the resulting fan and attach it with pins to the foam round, behind the heart.

Pleat an additional strip of net as high as the base and twice as long as it is around, then pin the pleated net around the base with straight pins pushed through tiny fabric flowers. Cover the top surface of the base with the tiny flowers in a similar manner, then stand a bride and groom in front of the heart for a striking effect.

6. If your wedding will be held during the Christmas season, you will have a wonderland of decorations to choose from. Visit the trim-a-tree section of almost any department store, and you will find a variety of tiny churches, sleighs, bells, and other miniatures that might be transformed into a wedding cake top with a holiday mood.

A smart woman I know chose a pair of china angels to top her cake, one an adorable little girl angel with an innocent grin, and the other a charming male cherub with a crooked halo and a large shiner. They were the talk of the town.

7. Another woman selected a charming china music box to top her cake. Featuring a pair of young lovers on a revolving base, the music box played "Lara's Theme" ("Somewhere My Love") as she cut the cake.

Something like this can be kept for all future brides in a family and brought out on anniversaries to bring back memories.

8. And if you are really a sentimental sort, ask your mother (or his) whatever became of the bride and groom from her wedding cake. Nancy used mine on her cake. With just a bit of sprucing up, they were good as new.

Now we're saving it for our younger daughter, Holly Sue, who has dibs on it.

9. If you're interested in starting a family tradition while saving some money, too, scout antique shops, curio counters, and boutiques for some figurines, a music box, or other trinket to top your cake. You may be surprised what you will find for under five dollars. The ready-made cake tops sold in bakeries will cost you twice or three times that amount.

10. Finally, if you don't see anything that really turns you on, you might try this. Scan the Yellow Pages of your phone book for a ceramic studio or glass blower. Either can create a bride and groom, pair of doves, wedding bells, or some other motif that could become a real family heirloom.

If you don't find a listing for either of these, check under amusement park headings, for most large amusement centers feature a glass blower's booth.

16
putting it
all together

My greatest hints and money-saving tips will be wasted on you unless you are able to coordinate them to create the exact look and mood you want most for your wedding day. To help you do just that, I have put together ten fabulous weddings for $300 or less, using ideas from previous chapters.

Study these model weddings carefully and you will find that, although they vary greatly in content, they are based on a simple formula that combines well-thought-out themes, carefully considered costumes, artful accessories, and beautifully balanced ideas to achieve a total look that can be kept completely within your budget.

The format I have selected for presenting these weddings to you includes the basics, those items that form the nucleus of the wedding both in content and cost: gowns, flowers, food, drink, and music. If you keep the expenditures for these items at a minimum, you will be able to add a myriad of romantic little touches without fear of running the tab up too much. If, however, you go overboard on any of these basics, you may wind up without funds for the little things that can make your wedding one that will be remembered long after countless others are forgotten.

Mix and Match

After you have considered the model weddings, take paper and pencil and thumb through the book again, noting the ideas that appeal most to you. Mix and match your favorites in outline form as I have, until your dream wedding begins to take shape. When you have found the combination that spells "YOU"—Yours, Original and Unique—you are on your way. (Keep in mind that prices are approximate.)

CHINESE WEDDING
$281.00

Item	How To	Cost
Wedding Gown	Floor-length mandarin-style dress, slit from bottom hem to knee and fashioned of white brocade.	$75.00
	Jeweled temple headdress from base purchased at costume shop, covered with pearls and bead-centered sequins.	$12.00
Attendants' Gowns	Short version of bride's gown in a pastel cotton satin or Chinese weave.	$30.00 each

Flowers	White China mums (six) with stems on and long satin streamers for bride.	$12.00
	A single large colored mum with a white bow and long streamers for the bridesmaids, or forget their flowers, using instead colored paper lanterns.	$2.00 each
Reception	Individual sesame cakes replace wedding cake. Buffet dinner featuring chicken chow mein (the soft kind), sweet and sour pork, mushrooms, oysters, and fortune cookies for everyone.	$150.00

Indoors, or out, this Chinese-style wedding reception is simply elegant. This is another ceremony in which the men of the wedding party may want to adopt the ethnic costume. A visit to Chinatown in any large metropolitan area will afford a variety of inexpensive decorations for the church and reception. Paper lanterns, temple bells, screens, and fans are great decorations, and you can even give an authentic scent to the ceremonies with incense.

Whether you will have to match the shoestring budget we have selected, or will have many times that amount to spend, you will find serving as your own wedding consultant rewarding in countless ways. Not the least of them is: what you want is what you get!

HEIRLOOM WEDDING
$158.00

Item	How To	Cost
Wedding Gown	Borrowed from Grandma, Mom or good friend (or purchased from a thrift shop). Veil as on page 87.	$00.00 $5.00
Attendants' Gowns	Made by each attendant, from simple floor-length patterns	$10.50 each

	trimmed to echo era of bride's gown. (Use a cotton fabric).	
Flower Girl	As above but in miniature.	$7.50
Flowers	Bride's bouquet is old fashioned nosegay of carnations and roses.	$10.00
	Attendants' flowers are smaller versions, featuring carnations and bachelor buttons or mums. These are easily made per instructions on page 102.	$5.00
Reception	Cake made from stacked sheet cakes as on page 176.	$35.00
	Prim's Champagne Punch, as on page 174. Enough for 50 guests.	$40.00
	Finger sandwiches, nuts, mints, dates, fresh fruit, fudge and other old-fashioned treats.	$45.00

Suggest home or church as setting. Invitations handwritten on old-fashioned notepaper by someone with old-fashioned good penmanship (maybe Grandma). Music should reflect era of bride's gown. A neat touch is to borrow a vintage car or other items of the era to carry out the theme; for example, dancing to the music of a borrowed gramophone doesn't cost a thing, but guests will long remember you for thinking of it and for adding a unique quality to your reception in that way.

HEAVENLY WEDDING
(fast and fabulous)
$135.00

Item	How To	Cost
Wedding Gown	Angel robe fashioned of white drapery satin per instructions	$17.00

	on page 80, or borrow a Job's Daughter robe and be a beautiful bride for free!	
Attendants' Gowns	Borrowed choir robes from your church or school. Each carries a tall taper tied with satin streamers in a complementary color. The only cost here is for candles and halos of daisies and baby's breath.	$3.00 each
Flowers	Halo of white roses and baby's breath gives you a truly angelic look. You carry a prayer book topped by a single white rose and a spray of heather fern.	$15.00
Reception	Cake of two half sheet cakes put together to form "Wedding Book" as on page 180, or angel food cake.	$25.00
	Mock champagne for a truly angelic touch—not a drop of alcohol. Enough for 50 guests. Finger sandwiches and never soggy appetizers.	$35.00
Music	An organist is a must for this ceremony, and you may have saved enough to have her or him perform at reception, too.	$40.00

If there are lots of brothers and sisters you'd like to have in the wedding party but nothing in the budget for gowns and rented tuxedo, this wedding is the solution. Simple and simply elegant, the effect of choir-robed attendants (both boys and girls) is smashing. As they stand with lighted tapers alongside the bride and groom, the picture is so perfect that guests are certain heaven couldn't be any better than this.

HAWAIIAN WEDDING
$140.00

Item	How To	Cost
Wedding Gown	White brocade styled in a Polynesian pattern, as suggested on page 77.	$25.00
Attendants' Gowns	Colorful cotton versions of the bride's gown, made at home or purchased from loungewear section of department store.	$15.00 each
Flowers	Hawaiian leis to be used as on page 96, Flowers for the hair.	$30.00
Reception	Export Punch, enough for 50.	$30.00
	Island hors d'oevres, enough for 50 guests, including shrimp balls, sweet and sour franks (pages 162, and 163) and chicken wings, fruit boat and poi aplenty.	$40.00

Suggest a garden, seashore, or lakeside setting in a warm month, and reception held on the spot. Invitations could be informal photo offset folders as on page 38, using a Hawaiian greeting or line from the Hawaiian Wedding Song to hint of the unique ceremony being planned. Recorded music is effective out-of-doors and easy, too, with today's portable tape players, yet it can set a romantic mood at no extra cost. Arrange reception gift table at luau level and invite guests to browse around it by winding receiving line past it, providing a punch stop along the way. If budget permits, a nice touch is a basket of fresh flowers for the bride to give blossoms from, with an aloha, as she is kissed in the reception line.

PEASANT WEDDING
$141.00

Item	How To	Cost
Wedding Gown	Make it of white flocked cotton with multicolored ribbon trim	$12.00

from a pattern using elastic for fitting.

Make a headpiece from multi-colored flowers and ribbon streamers, as on page 85. $3.50

Attendants' Gowns   Bright cotton print gowns (a patchwork print is fun) fashioned like the bride's, but without the lavish ribbon trim. Each wears a triangle scarf tied under the chin. $7.50 each

Flowers   Fresh cut flowers with stems still on—mums, daisies, bachelor buttons, and the like—carried in the arms as though just picked. $10.00

Bridesmaids carry small bunches of same flowers, with shorter stems tied with satin streamers. $3.00

Reception   A park meadow or hillside is perfect for both wedding and reception, but an intimate chapel with a pretty garden is just as nice if your ideas are more conventional. $105.00

Forget the traditional cake and reception fare, selecting instead individual date or other fruit cakes heaped in flower-trimmed wicker baskets, to be passed by bridesmaids, and wine to be served by the ushers in gallon jugs piled high in a decorated wheelbarrow. Serve also chunk cheese, fruit and nuts.

Invite all talented guests to bring their guitars, flutes, zith-

ers, or whatever to add music
and gaiety to the occasion.

Your mother won't like this idea at first, but once she sees you in
your fresh-as-a-daisy gown, she'll be certain you're on the right
track.

This is a perfect wedding for those who want to recite poetry,
sing, or dance during the ceremony, or be married in a circle of
friends with all guests joining hands around them to symbolize everlasting love.

ROCK 'N' ROLL WEDDING
$189.00

Item	*How To*	*Cost*
Wedding Gown	Minilength gown of white table lace, as on page 82. White lace tights. Briefest veil attached to satin bow with hem-length streamers. White boots.	$25.00
Attendants' Gowns	Circle minigowns like that of the bride but in hot colors, such as shocking pink, turquoise, lavender (very fifties). Matching tights and satin bows for the hair. Matching boots.	$20.00 each
Flowers	Pin a large "cabbage" rose to tiny drawstring purses, carried in lieu of bouquets.	$4.00 each
Reception	Concert-style, outdoors in an amphitheater or park. Lots of beer, hot dogs, chili, and rock 'n' roll music. Top the cake with a bride and groom standing in front of a 45 rpm record of the couple's favorite song or group. (Invite guests to come in fifties clothing if they desire.)	$140.00

Ceremony	Vows could be lyrics of "Love Me Tender." Replace wedding march with soft rock sounds.

More Model Weddings

As I explained in Chapter 1, the popularity of ethnic weddings—Mexican, African, Chinese, Japanese, and native American—is growing rapidly.

Putting together such a wedding can be both fun and profitable. By sticking to the costumes and customs of your family heritage, you have a delightful excuse to do the inexpensive and depart from the costly norm.

Doubling the budget we used for the first sample weddings, I have prepared five more, all with ethnic overtones and easily put together for under $300.00.

ACAPULCO WEDDING
$225.00

Item	How To	Cost
Wedding Gown	Fashioned of unbleached muslin and cotton lace. Worn with lace mantilla or silk rebozo.	$30.00
Attendants' Gowns	White peasant blouse and gaily colored floor-length full skirt with cotton lace insets.	$25.00 each
Flowers	Fresh cut daisies, dahlias, mums, and lemon leaves with the stems on, for the bride to carry in her left arm as she clasps her fingers through a rosary. Just rosaries for the attendants.	$20.00
Reception	Mexican wedding cakes (individual) heaped in wicker baskets, on page 170.	$150.00

Cerveza (that's beer) in bottles,
and plenty of it. Or Border
Buttermilk as on page 175.
Tamale pie, guacamole, refried
beans (in quantity) served with
tortilla strips crisply fried (or
corn chips) to dip, scoop, or just
munch.

This is a delightful wedding for couples in the Southwest, where
many settings offer authentic Mexican architecture and where often Mexican clothing can be purchased very inexpensively in border towns. The groom will look special in an embroidered wedding
shirt, about $15. The costumes are easy to make, however, and fea-
ture inexpensive materials. To spark the reception, stack the record
player with mariachi music, adorn the hall with brightly colored
paper flowers and piñatas (as on page 123), and let the groom break
one filed with fortunes or candy. Baskets of blown eggs refilled
with confetti are distributed to the children to break and shower
the couple with as they leave on their honeymoon.

JAPANESE WEDDING
$248.75

Item	How To	Cost
Wedding Gown	White silk (or polyester) kimono with silver obi, worn with flowers and jeweled chopsticks in the hair.	$65.00
Attendants' Gowns	Brightly printed cotton kimonos with contrasting obis.	$20.00
Flowers	A pair of large mums on a white silk fan with satin streamers for the bride.	$22.50
	Smaller colored mums attached to glass and wind chimes as on page 98.	$1.25 each

Reception	Pagoda-style cake. Sake wine, jumbo shrimp and hot sauce, waterchestnut rumaki, stuffed mushrooms, and tangy seafood appetizers.	$140.00

Japanese weddings are traditionally held outdoors, in a park or garden setting of lush splendor, so eat your heart out if you live in the desert or the frozen North. To add to the setting, hang a myriad of different wind chimes from the trees and let them provide "natural" music for the ceremony, along with those your attendants will carry. If no one you know plays traditional Japanese instruments, there are recordings both on tape and long-playing albums that can provide authentic music during the reception.

NATIVE AMERICAN WEDDING
$287.50

Item	*How To*	*Cost*
Wedding Gown	Fringed rawhide shift embroidered with beads, easy to make at home without a sewing machine. Also beaded headband. (You can cut the cost to a fourth by using vinyl instead of leather, and you'll have your choice of colors, too.) See page 81.	$150.00
Attendants' Gowns	Similar long fringed gowns with less beading and fashioned of vinyl. All wear beaded headbands.	$30.00 each
Flowers	Forget them, Have attendants carry torches (candles) instead, to be lit from the ceremonial fire.	$2.50
Reception	If you want to adapt conventional wedding fare to your In-	$105.00

dian theme, however, try a
teepee cake with a pair of Indian dolls replacing the bride
and groom, label the punch
bowl "firewater," and serve
candied nutmeats and fruits in
Indian pottery or baskets (if
you can afford them).

The costumes of the Plains Indians with their long fringed gowns
make striking wedding attire. Weather permitting, the groom and
ushers might go bare-chested and wear leather pants with loincloths or (if they are really daring) loincloths alone. The setting
should be out-of-doors somewhere where campfires are permitted.
Dusk is a good time for such a ceremony, with guests gathered
around the fire. For a truly dramatic entrance, ushers could sound
drums, and the groom could enter on horseback.

BLACK CULTURE WEDDING
$195.00

Item	*How To*	*Cost*
Wedding Gown	From Instant Pattern 1 or 2 on page 78, in a bright African print. Matching fabric headpiece.	$20.00
Attendants' Gowns	Also from instant patterns but in solid color.	$15.00
Flowers	Bride and attendants carry baskets of flowers on their heads.	$35.00
Reception	Black is beautiful, so be daring and dig a devil's food wedding cake frosted and decorated in deep dark chocolate.	$125.00
	Plan a buffet that is easy to fix and serve, starting with baked ham, cheese grits, and corn muffins. Add southern fried chicken if budget permits.	
	Top it off with a Rosé Punch.	

Costumes for the Black Culture wedding can be adapted for the male members of the wedding party, too, if you use Pattern 2. An entire wedding party dressed in these colorful, flowing robes is indeed a spectacular and impressive sight.

Decorate the reception room with lengths of print fabric and with the baskets of flowers the women wore on their heads during the wedding.

Ask talented friends to bring their musical instruments to the reception and stage a jam session if there is room for dancing.

17

the budget bride's buying guide

Budget-conscious brides reading this book have been warned to leave checkbooks at home when checking out bridal boutiques. What follows here is a listing of the kinds of shops and other sources for bridal wares you will want to patronize as you plan your wedding.

Do bring your checkbook when you visit these stores, and in some cases it is advisable to bring cash, as some shops do not accept personal checks.

Some Surprising Sources

Due to the fact that an individual listing of stores and addresses would be too lengthy to present here, I have simply listed the type of establishment likely to carry the wanted items. Before you set out in search of them, let your fingers do the walking through the Yellow Pages and locate the vendors nearest you. This will provide an additional savings of both money and time. And, remember, every penny counts!

RINGS

Pawn Shops
Jewelry-Making Classes

Antique Dealers
Gemologists

Estate Sales
Jewelry Wholesalers
Art Festivals

Goldsmiths
Classified Ads

BRIDAL GOWNS

Thrift Shops
Classified Ads
Garment Districts (Wholesalers)
Manufacturers' Outlets

Sewing Classes
Second-Hand Stores
Garage Sales
Seamstresses

FLOWERS

Super Market Produce
Managers
Flower-Arranging Classes
Wholesale Flower Markets
Nurseries

Garden Clubs
Green-Thumbed Friends
Independent Growers

PHOTOGRAPHERS

Local Newspapers
Police Department
Photography Classes

Public Relations Firms
Photography Clubs
Local Magazines

DECORATIONS

Florist Supply Houses*
Nurseries
Religious Goods Dealers
Arts and Crafts Shops
Religious Book Stores

Restaurant and Catering Supply
Houses
Paper Goods Wholesalers
Churches
Party Shops

*These carry everything you'll need to prepare your own bridal bouquets, altar arrangements, and the like. Many also carry disposable aisle runners and inexpensive paper goods, and larger ones also generally rent candelabras, standing baskets, and so on.

INVITATIONS

Religious Book Stores
Speedy Printers

Paper Wholesalers
Graphics Classes

Religious Goods Dealers*   Party Shops

*These carry such things as wedding program "blanks" on which you can imprint your own wedding message and information. And they have a variety of other items suitable as wedding stationery.

TABLES AND CHAIRS

Fire Department*   Women's Clubs

City Recreation Departments   School Districts

Mortuaries*

*These frequently lend folding chairs and tables free of charge as a community service.

"LIMOUSINES"

Mortuaries   Bus Companies*

Custom Car Clubs*   Riding Stables*

Antique Car Clubs*

*These offer specialty vehicles like unique cars, horse-drawn carriages, double-decker buses and minibuses for the exotic getaway. A fire truck, police car, or the like, if appropriate to your occupation or that of your spouse, can often be arranged in the name of "love" if you know the right people and are willing to make a donation to the fire or police benevolent association.

VOCALISTS/MUSIC/ENTERTAINMENT

Musicians' Union Local*   Community Choirs

Community Bands   Music Schools

Local Piano Bars**   Restaurants

Barbershop Quartets†   Churches

College Music Departments   Sweet Adelines†

Friends   Nightclubs

*You'll get quality musicians here, but you'll have to pay union scale. If you contact the musicians in their places of work—restaurants, piano bars, or nightclubs—you may interest them in moonlighting for your wedding or reception at a reduced fee (which they won't have to report to their union if they are members).

**These are outstanding sources for vocalists, as most are frequented by "amateur" singers who have had a lot of practice and are quite professional in their presentation. Many are flattered to be asked to perform and will ask little or nothing for their services. Also, most of the pianists play weekend weddings (daytimes) to add to their incomes.

†These are performing groups that provide delightful harmony and are accustomed to performing a cappella (without accompaniment), which is ideal if you want music at an outdoor wedding where no electricity is available or where a piano or organ would be impractical. They usually have delightful costumes, as well.

NONRELIGIOUS OR NONSECTARIAN WEDDING SITES

Cemetery or Mortuary Chapels*　　Beaches*

Auditoriums**　　　　　　　　　Public Parks*

Rose Gardens*　　　　　　　　　Arboretums*

Homes of Family/Friends*　　　Theaters**

Community Centers*　　　　　　Clubhouses**

Union Halls†　　　　　　　　　Local Monuments*

Country Clubs**　　　　　　　Hotels**

National Monuments*　　　　　Campgrounds*

Scout Houses†　　　　　　　　Historical Sites*

Picnic Grounds*

*These are generally free or very low cost.

**These can be quite expensive. Shop carefully and ask about extras or hidden costs—corkage, for example.

†These are more moderately priced but may have some restrictions or need to be reserved considerably in advance.

For additional ideas, consult the where-to-do-it section of this book!

ACCESSORIES

Arts-and-Crafts Fairs*　　　Sewing Classes**

Church Bazaars*　　　　　　Hobby Shops**

Floral Supply Houses**　　　Hobby Clubs**

*These are excellent sources for things such as popular quilted photo albums, picture frames, unique decorations, and items to double as cake tops.

**These carry items you'll need to make accessories such as garters, decorated fans, headpieces, and floral baskets if you decide to do it yourself.

ARTISTS/ARTISANS

Community Colleges*　　　Specialty/Hobby/Clubs**

Trade Schools**　　　　　Recreation Departments*

Adult School Classes*   Art Societies*

*These can provide you with calligraphers, printers, floral arrangers, portrait artists, seamstresses, musicians, vocalists, glass blowers, student photographers, and so on.

**These, depending upon the specialty, can provide low-cost hair stylists, manicurists, graphic artists, illustrators, printers, student caterers, amateur photographers, musicians, decorators, waiters, bartenders, and so on.

18
where to do it

Finding a site for your wedding has been discussed earlier in this book. The following directory of way-out wedding locations is offered here to give you courage to do it where *you* want to in spite of criticism from family and friends.

Gathered from the desks of women's editors across the nation, most of these locations have already served as wedding sites at one time or another.

Some are traditional churches, temples, or chapels with unusual architecture or decor. Others, however, run the gamut from underground caverns and desert ghost towns to woodland waterfalls and public parks.

ALABAMA

St. Michael and All Angels Episcopal Church in Anniston, with its 95-foot tower, rectory, parish house and assembly room of Norman Gothic architecture executed in native stone, is one of the outstanding buildings of the South. Its interior is highlighted by carved woodwork, stained-glass windows, and a marble altar. A very elegant setting for a large formal wedding.

For a less formal but equally charming site, try *Bienville Square,* a beautiful little park with a myriad of azaleas and live oaks, located in the business district of *Mobile.* Open to the public

free. Daily observation for a week or so would indicate what days and hours you could probably have the square virtually to yourself.

ALASKA

The Log Church at Auke Lake just outside *Juneau* is perhaps the most unusual church in the United States. A wall of glass behind the pulpit affords wedding guests a view of Mendenhall Glacier and the mountains around the Juneau ice fields. You'll look hard to find any natural wonder quite as spectacular.

St. Michael's Cathedral (Greek Orthodox) in *Sitka* was built in 1841. It burned to the ground in 1966 and was recently rebuilt. Services are again being conducted, using treasures rescued at the time of the fire, wedding crowns once worn by Russian princesses, and other ceremonial items originally brought from Russia by Father John Veniamenov.

ARIZONA

There's a rugged stone observation tower overlooking the *Grand Canyon*, and there's room at the top for an intimate wedding ceremony looking out over one of the natural wonders of the world. Arrangements may be made through the Visitor Center, where you will also be able to arrange a day and time when the tower is virtually deserted.

Desert lovers will enjoy *Organ Pipe Cactus National Monument* as a site for their nuptials. No pipe organs here though, just the wind whistling across the 40-acre monument located on State 85, about 35 miles south of Ajo.

ARKANSAS

Enrico Pandolfini fashioned the Stations of the Cross in Italian marble along the walkway from the bell tower of *St. Elizabeth Church,* which is located just off U.S. 62 city route on Crescent Drive in *Eureka Springs.* Another unique feature of this church where all denominations are welcome is its entrance, through the bell tower.

Christ of the Ozarks, just three miles east of Eureka Springs on U.S. 62, towers seven stories above Magnetic Mountain. The outstretched arms of the statue measure 65 feet across, giving the huge work of art the look of a giant cross.

Say your vows standing in the shadow of the Lord for a really heavenly outdoor ceremony. Admission is free.

CALIFORNIA

California's chain of old missions offers 22 picturesque sites from San Diego north to the San Francisco Bay area. All relics of the days of Spanish occupation, many of the missions are operated as state parks or historical sites, and most are easily accessible on well-kept roads. Some have moderate admission fees, and others simply welcome donations. See the mission directors for wedding details.

The vast state park system and several national parks afford a myriad of outdoor settings ranging from rugged coastlines to dense giant redwood groves. One of my favorite places and a perfect wedding spot is *Muir Woods National Monument,* 17 miles northwest of San Francisco via the Golden Gate Bridge and State Highway 1. Parking space is ample at the monument's edge; however, no cars are permitted inside. This is one of the most beautiful and accessible of the famous redwood groves. Here your wedding party can

cross a picturesque foot bridge to watch you exchange your vows as the sun filters through the trees and creates the look of an outdoor cathedral.

COLORADO

"Pike's Peak or Bust!" was the call of the pioneers. But many engaged Colorado couples have set their sights on beautiful snow-covered *Pike's Peak* with equal fervor when making wedding plans.

Those who like the warmer regions head for *Great Sand Dunes National Monument,* where a Visitor Center offers many possible wedding sites of an unusual nature.

And if the name's the game you're playing in picking a wedding site, how about *Miracle Rock,* 25 miles southwest through Colorado National Monument outside of *Grand Junction?*

CONNECTICUT

An Ionic portico and domed ceiling dominate the *Church of Christ Congregational* in *Milford.* Founded in 1693 and built in 1823, it represents one of the earliest organized religious groups in the country and is a charming place for a super traditional ceremony.

For the more avant-garde, *Hubbard Park,* about two miles west of *Meriden* on U.S. 6-A, is a picturesque 900-acre park in the Hanging Hills. Select *Castle Craig,* a stone observation tower, as a backdrop for a beautiful summer ceremony outdoors.

DELAWARE

In the town of *Frederica* is *Barratt's Chapel,* the cradle of Methodism in America. There in 1784 the sacraments were first administered in this quaint chapel. There is a museum next door where wedding information may be obtained.

Bringhurst Woods at Shipley and Washington Streets in *Wilmington* is a delightful wooded area preserved in its natural state. It provides an ideal setting for a simple outdoor ceremony in good weather, and picnicking is allowed if you want to plan a basket supper reception.

FLORIDA

Swaying palms beckon from deserted white sandy beaches on many of Florida's fabulous keys. Take the causeway and drive out to *Key West* or pick a spot somewhere between there and the mainland where wedding guests could shed their shoes and dip their feet in the warm Gulf with you and your husband-to-be as you recite your vows.

Or, if you've saved enough by doing yourself what you might have had to pay others handsomely for (by planning your wedding with this handy guide), charter a boat—there are even some old sailing vessels available—in Miami and say your vows at sea. Make certain, however, that if the captain performs them they are good for longer than just the duration of the cruise!

GEORGIA

In *Atlanta* the bells of Stone Mountain in *Stone Mountain Park* offer daily concerts that could provide free music for your wedding. Give your hand to him at the base of the 13-story tower, which is the focal point of the park. Then invite guests to join you for a reception aboard the riverboat *Robert E. Lee,* which offers lake cruises during the summer months.

Outside the tiny town of *Midway* (population 200) is one of Georgia's most historic churches, erected in 1792 and yielding two signers of the Declaration of Independence, two Revolutionary War

generals and a United States senator. Services are held in *The Midway Church* only on Memorial Day now, but keys are available year-round at the town's service station, where you can talk over wedding arrangements with the custodian of the church.

HAWAII

Travel by boat with your wedding guests to the fabled *Fern Grotto*, where "Hawaii Five-O" star James MacArthur and many others have wed.

Wear orchid leis and colorful island attire for this ceremony, highlighted, perhaps, by the singing of the Hawaiian Wedding Song, which echos through the grotto ethereally. The grotto is on *Kauai,* where you will also find another beautiful wedding spot, the *Hanalei Plantation,* where the motion picture *South Pacific* was filmed.

Driving along the *Kona Coast,* you will spot tiny white *St. Benedict's Church,* the first Catholic church on the island of *Hawaii,* with seating for scarcely a dozen wedding guests. If you're planning to wed in the Islands but haven't many friends or relatives there, this minichapel might be just what the preacher ordered for a quiet, intimate ceremony.

After the knot has been tied, honeymoon island-style in a thatched hut at the Cocoa Palms Plantation, where restrooms are open to the sky above and fixtures are fashioned from sea shells.

IDAHO

Got a long wedding list? The *Cathedral of the Rockies* can accommodate even the largest wedding, for it fills a complete city block from Franklin and Hay Streets between 11th and 12th Streets. An artistic array of stained-glass windows dominates the structure. It is located in *Boise*.

Also in Boise is *Ann Morrison Memorial Park*, between Capitol Boulevard and 16th Street on the south bank of the Boise River. It features an unusual illuminated fountain and flower gardens, perfect for an al fresco wedding on a warm summer evening.

ILLINOIS

U.S. 460 leads through *Belleville* to the *National Shrine of Our Lady of the Snows,* where the Roman legions could assemble for a wedding and still leave room for party crashers. Featuring an amphitheater that seats 20,000 as well as meditation areas that in-

clude the Stations of the Cross and a replica of the grotto at
Lourdes, it is, to say the least, spectacular. Skip the pilgrimage season from May to October, though, and opt for a time when wedding
guests won't get lost among the pilgrims.

A 72-bell carillon chimes from the tower of the *Rockefeller Memorial Chapel* at the *University of Chicago.* What better place to
give a low-cost wedding a note of prestige!

INDIANA

New Harmony is the setting of two distinctly different and beautiful
wedding sites. The first is known as *"The Labyrinth,"* a garden
maze which is a reproduction of the original Harmonist labyrinth.
It is part of the New Harmony State Memorial.

Also on the grounds is the unique *Roofless Church* at North
and Main Streets. This nonsectarian chapel features a dome by ar-
chitect Philip Johnson and a bronze sculpture, "Descent of the Holy
Spirit," by Jacques Lipchitz.

IOWA

Courthouse Square offers a spectacular setting in *Jefferson,* for the
Mahanay Memorial Carillon Tower is located here, along with a
128-foot high observation deck that can be reached by elevator. If
your wedding guest list is small, soar to the observation deck for a
ceremony in the sky and a carillon concert in the bargain.

If you're a Quaker, you'll want to explore the possibility of
holding your wedding in the restored *Quaker Meeting House* on the
grounds of the Herbert Hoover National Historic Site in *West Bend.*
It's the place of worship used by the late President Herbert Hoover
as a child.

KANSAS

If you can pronounce the name of the town, better use the telephone for your wedding invitations, because no printer will get this
one right the first time. It's *Osawatomie,* where the *Old Stone Congregational Church,* dedicated in 1861, stands at Sixth and Parker

Streets. An all-faith place of worship, it's also a spot with unique atmosphere.

Ancestors from Holland? In *Smith Center* the *City Park* contains one of only two Dutch windmills still standing in Kansas. What a neat place to stage your wedding ceremony, wearing wooden shoes and entering, perhaps, to the strains of "Home on the Range," which was composed in Smith Center.

KENTUCKY

Sixty-two art masterpieces donated by Louis Philippe of France in 1797 adorn *St. Joseph's Cathedral* in *Bardstown*. They include the work of such masters as Murillo, Rubens, Jacob Hast, van Bree, Van Dyck, and the van Eyck brothers. What a place for artists or art lovers to wed.

One of the world's largest stained-glass windows is a dominant feature of the *Basilica of the Assumption in Covington* at 12th and Madison Streets. Modeled after the famed Notre Dame of Paris, this church would do justice to the wedding of a queen.

LOUISIANA

Jackson Square in the heart of the French Quarter in *New Orleans* is a romantic European-like setting for a spring or summer wedding. The focal point of the square is Clark Mills' heroic equestrian bronze of Andrew Jackson. At the base of the statue is an inscription as fitting for a wedding as it was during the occupation of the city during the Civil War. It says, "This Union Must and Shall Be Preserved."

What may be the nation's smallest church is located at *Paque-*

mine and called the *Chapel of the Madonna.* Just six feet wide and eight feet long, it contains an altar and five chairs and allows just enough room for the priest and an acolyte during the ceremony.

MAINE

Climb *Mount David,* a rocky knoll on the *Bates College* campus and give wedding guests an uninterrupted view of the Androscoggen Valley and the Blue Mountains as they wait for you to repeat your vows. Select a fair weather month for your wedding if you pick this spot, however.

Delicate paneling and graceful design make the *Old Church* at *Kittery* a memorable wedding site. A First Congregational church, it was erected in 1730 and remodeled in 1874.

MARYLAND

The *Dunkard Church* on the grounds of the *Antietam National Battlefield* was first built in 1852 and offered regular services until 1916, when it fell into disrepair. It has been reconstructed, however, as a landmark on this historic site, and it stands just opposite the Visitor Center, where wedding inquiries may be made.

In historic *Baltimore* the *Lloyd Street Synagogue* is one of the earliest in the nation. Built in 1845, it is still in good repair and open for inspection the first and third Sundays of each month, free.

MASSACHUSETTS

The Mother Church of the *First Church of Christ Scientist* is located in *Boston* off Massachusetts Avenue near Huntington Avenue. It is the hub of the Christian Science movement in the world.

The public garden behind the *Boston Common* is charmingly landscaped and contains many noted pieces of statuary as well as swan boats which operate mid-April to the last Sunday in September. What could be more romantic?

MICHIGAN

In *Mio,* Michigan, on State 72 just west of Highway 33, is *Our Lady of the Woods Shrine,* which contains replicas of famous Roman Catholic shrines in a splendid outdoor setting. It is open all year, free.

At the end of *Pictured Rocks Trail,* overlooking *Lake Superior,* is *Miners Castle*—a rock formation that might provide an unusual wedding setting. The trail and castle rock are open daily from early spring to late fall, free during daylight hours.

MINNESOTA

What woman wouldn't like to say she began her marriage in *Harmony* or better yet, in romantic *Niagara Cave?* Just two miles south of State 139 and then two miles west is this interesting formation with its crystal chapel and 60-foot waterfall 150 feet underground. There's an admission fee, but it is nominal, and, if your wedding party is small, well worth it.

In *St. Cloud, St. John's Abbey,* on the grounds of a university of the same name, is a contemporary-style church noted for its 112-bell banner, designed by Marcel Breuer. Inquire about weddings at the reception center.

MISSISSIPPI

The *Church of the Redeemer* at Bellman Street and East Beach Boulevard in *Biloxi* is the Episcopal church where Jefferson Davis worshipped. It contains four memorial windows dedicated to his family, and the family pew is marked with a silver plate and draped with the flag of the Confederacy. If you're a true daughter of the South, you will surely want to be married here.

Holmes County State Park, five miles south of *Durant,* offers 463 acres of woods encircling a picturesque lake which is easily reached by U.S. 51. A perfect setting can be found in any one of a hundred places around the lake or in these charming woods.

MISSOURI

Mark Twain State Park, located about a half-mile outside the city of *Florida* on State Highway 107, is a beautiful spot named for the beloved American author. Walking along these nature trails, you can easily imagine Huck Finn and Becky Thatcher all grown-up and repeating wedding vows under a tree. Plenty of room, too, for a picnic-style reception in this 1,192-acre wonderland.

Indian Point, about ten miles outside *Branson* on State Highway 76 by way of country road 76-60, is a perfect wedding spot if

214

you're the Pocahontas type. A sundown ceremony at the lake's edge here could be followed with a fireside pow-wow replacing the more traditional reception. *Table Rock Reservoir* provides a lovely lake shore for such plans.

MONTANA

Traveling out of *Anaconda* on U.S. 10-A you arrive at a lush, natural setting worthy of the world's first lovers, Adam and Eve. It's *Lost Creek Falls,* where sparkling water cascades over sheet rock in a setting of willows, aspens, and evergreens. Picnicking and camping are allowed, and you will find ample space there for both wedding and reception, with Lost Creek sounding its natural music as it rushes through a 3,000-foot gorge nearby.

The famous cathedral at Cologne, Germany inspired *St. Helena Cathedral* here in *Helena.* A handsome Gothic structure located on Warren Street between Ninth and Tenth Avenues, it is furnished inside with marble appointments and elegant stained-glass windows.

NEBRASKA

St. Cecilia's Cathedral on 40th Street in *Omaha* is a lovely religious setting at any time of the year, but when covered with a layer of new-fallen snow, it's particularly picturesque. In conjunction with

the larger facility is *Our Lady of Nebraska Chapel,* perfect for small
ceremonies.

Valentine, Nebraska would look nice on any wedding invitation but the name isn't this town's only drawing card. Located here
is *Fort Niobrara National Wildlife Refuge,* a scant five miles out of
town on State 12. A picnic area, scenic trails, and pastures all afford pretty spots for an outdoor wedding in good weather months.

NEVADA

Both *Las Vegas* and *Reno* offer a myriad of wedding chapels and
packaged honeymoon plans. The services of such commercial establishments should not be overlooked if you live near such a city, for
many of the chapels are beautifully appointed and include flowers
and music and the like at nominal costs. Do some comparative
shopping if you plan to marry in one of them, however, for prices
vary considerably.

Washoe County Courthouse on South Virginia Street in *Reno*
is known as the busiest divorce court in the country, but it is interesting to note that there are nearly seven times as many couples being married there as being divorced.

Athens it ain't but *Rhyolite,* Nevada is a picturesque city of
ruins that would be an interesting background for a wedding with
an ancient Greek or Roman theme. Once thought destined to be the
capital of Nevada, the mining town of 12,000 inhabitants today is
virtually deserted, its citizens having left when the gold and silver
ran out.

Better bring picnic lunches for your guests, or commandeer a
catering truck along the way, for there is little other than a most
ususual setting offered here.

NEW HAMPSHIRE

Rhododendron State Park, a mass of colorful flowers in the sum-
mertime, is easily accessible and provides a perfect setting for nature lovers' nuptials. Located 2½ miles outside the small town of
Fitzwilliam, it features a 16-acre bed of wild rhododendrons, which
is usually in full bloom by mid-July.

St. John's Church on Chapel Street in *Portsmouth* houses the

nation's oldest known pipe organ and one of the four known copies of the "Vinegar Bible," so named for a misspelling of the word 'vineyard' contained in it. The bible was printed in 1717, almost a century before the church was erected in 1807.

NEW JERSEY

Princeton University Chapel is one of the largest chapels in America. Featuring fine stained glass and a pulpit and lectern brought from France, it offers an elegant setting for a formal wedding of some proportions.

In Newark is the Catholic *Cathedral of the Sacred Heart* that rivals the famed Westminster Abbey and is reminiscent of the Basilica at Rheims. Among its fantastic appointments are more than 200 stained-glass windows, cast bronze doors, 14 bells cast in Italy, and towers reaching 232 feet into the sky. If the United States were an empire, its royalty would certainly marry here.

NEW MEXICO

Carlsbad Caverns, with its colorful formations, offers one of the most unique wedding sites anywhere in the Southwest. Located just outside *Whites City,* it is open all year and offers natural rooms of all sizes for a truly underground wedding.

A perfect spot for the wedding of two dedicated backpackers is *Angels Peak.* This recreation area, 13 miles southeast of *Bloomfield* on State Highway 44, then about five miles down a dirt road, includes 495 acres supervised by the Bureau of Land Management. A haven for hikers—if you'd marry with your boots on, this is the place.

NEW YORK

Montour Falls occupies the site of *Catharines Town*, named for Queen Catharine Montour of the Iroquois Indian Nation. A score of waterfalls flows through the seven glens which surround the town. Havana Glen, with more than 30 falls, is a recreational area where you might stage a lovely Indian-style ceremony.

St. Peter's Episcopal Church in *Albany* at State and Lodge Streets is an elegant example of French Gothic architecture, one of the best in this country. It boasts a communion service presented by Queen Anne in 1712 and features magnificent stained-glass windows.

NORTH CAROLINA

If a civil ceremony is your preference, how about one performed in the oldest courthouse in use in the state? Built in 1767, *Chowan County Courthouse* in *Edenton* fits the picture. The paneling and finishing of the walls in many rooms, particularly on the second floor, are worth noting. If you prefer an outdoor wedding, ask a judge to step out to the *Edenton public green* that slopes to Edenton Bay. Once this area was equipped with stocks and pillory where criminals paid for their crimes, but it could be a charming spot for a simple ceremony.

Looking Glass Rock and Falls in the *Pisgah National Forest* on U.S. 276 are located about six miles from the forest entrance. The rock, which glistens like a mirror, is the largest monolith in the southern Appalachians. Select this scenic site for the ceremony, then move on to *"Pink Beds,"* an azalea garden about four miles down the road, for a picnic reception.

NORTH DAKOTA

The capital of North Dakota, at *Bismarck,* features a statue in memory of the wife of a Shoshone interpreter of the Lewis and Clark expedition. If there's Indian blood in your veins, as is the case with so many North Dakotans, why not exchange vows with your prospective chief in the shadow of this most famous Indian wife?

There's an outdoor theater in *Medora* that's used only July 1 through Labor Day. They put on musical shows there in the evenings during that brief season. Does that give you any ideas?

OHIO

In *Dayton,* you can save the cost of musicians by marrying in *Carillon Park* some Sunday evening at 7 P.M. (June through August) or at 5 P.M. (September through October). That's when special concerts are held in this public park located on U.S. 25 at Patterson Boulevard.

You'll find some marvelous outdoor settings for your wedding within the 61-acre park which has a transportation theme and features exhibits, including a restored Wright Brothers' airplane and an early locomotive.

In *Cleveland* the *Cultural Gardens* in *Rockefeller Park* between Superior and St. Clair Avenues offer many wedding possibilities. Here, more than 20 ethnic groups are creating gardens to represent their native lands. You're sure to find one that suits your heritage.

OKLAHOMA

A total of 100 acres of beautiful gardens, lakes, and lily ponds awaits brides yearning for an outdoor wedding in the city of *Muskogee*, where *Honor Heights Park* is located. The azaleas are particularly pretty in April.

In *Tulsa*, many brides have selected the *First Methodist Church*, with its perpendicular Tudor Gothic architecture executed in native limestone, as the site of their weddings. It is located at 11th and Boulder Streets.

OREGON

Bridal Veil—just think how that would look on your wedding invitations. This spot is more than just a pretty name, however. A 332-acre park, *Shepperd's Dell*, is located here on the *Columbia River Scenic Route, U.S. 30.* Many interesting rock formations provide natural altars if you are imaginative, and a waterfall sounds musically and is easily accessible by a well-traveled trail.

Cave Junction is the turnoff to get to a dual-purpose wedding site or honeymoon home. The *Oregon Caves* are located just 20 miles east of the Junction, and the marble halls that abound underground contain two rooms that can serve as chapels, one with spiral stairs perfect for a bride to descend.

If you don't want a real underground wedding, there is a

charming lodge here, too, with gabled roof and lobby overlooking a crystal clear mountain pool. In winter this quaint building glistens with icicles and wears a beautiful mantle of snow.

Send wedding guests packing after the reception in front of a huge lobby fireplace and then stay on for awhile for an unforgettable honeymoon.

PENNSYLVANIA

Be married in *Bethlehem* without leaving the United States. There is an ancient church here, too—though not quite as old as those of the Holy Land. This quaint chapel, called *The Old Chapel,* is said to have been the third structure erected in the town. Built in 1751 with thick walls and massive buttresses, it is now used only for weddings and special occasions.

Hellertown is the home of the *Lost River Caverns,* the perfect setting for the marriage of two spelunkers (cave explorers). For a small admission fee you and your wedding guests can descend to a limestone chamber which serves as a chapel and is complete with photo flood lighting.

RHODE ISLAND

Touro Synagogue in *Newport,* located at 72 Touro Street, is a national historic site—the oldest synagogue in the United States. Opened in 1763, it has been in operation almost continually since then and still has services at 7:30 P.M. on Fridays and 9 A.M. on Saturdays.

The historic nature of this site isn't its only recommendation, however. The interior of the building is considered an architectural wonder of the era in which it was constructed.

Providence boasts magnificent 425-acre *Roger Williams Park,* where a chain of lakes covering 140 acres offers a myriad of possible wedding sites, perfect in spring and summer months. In May, tulips and azaleas abound; later in the year chrysanthemums offer a profusion of color and even in winter the park is alive with Christmas flowers.

You reach the park via the Elmwood Avenue exit of I-95 or by way of U.S. 1, Broad Street and Park Avenue.

SOUTH CAROLINA

St. Michael's Episcopal Church of *Charleston,* with its Palladian Doric portico and 186-foot high steeple, was built in 1751. George Washington, Lafayette, and Robert E. Lee attended services here.

The clock in the tower has marked the time since 1764, and the sanctuary remains open daily. If you're a DAR type, this is your place.

Edisto Gardens, a city park in *Orangeburg* on the banks of the North Edisto River, contains 85 acres of moss-draped oaks, camellias, and other blooming shrubs and flowers that are particularly pretty in March and April. The park is open free to the public and offers plenty of room for a reception, too.

SOUTH DAKOTA

Mount Rushmore National Monument offers several possible wedding sites but the outdoor amphitheater where lectures are heard in the evenings would be a nice spot. Check with the Visitor Center for arrangements.

Spearfish, the home of the Black Hills Passion Play, has a similar amphitheater just west of town, overlooking Lookout Mountain in the distance. Contact Passion Play Headquarters for days and dates the facility is not in use.

TENNESSEE

The *Parthenon* in *Nashville*? It may sound surprising, but it's true. Located in Centennial Park on West End Avenue, it's the only full-sized replica of the Parthenon on the Acropolis at Athens.

Floodlighted at night, it is a particularly striking sight.

Rather than seeking a wedding inside, where the James Cowan art collection resides, let this spectacular piece of architecture serve as the backdrop to an outdoor ceremony on a warm summer evening.

Cades Cove in the *Great Smoky Mountains National Park,* off Little River Road on the Tennessee side of the park, provides a perfect setting for a Pioneer Theme Wedding. Here a completely restored pioneer village is open to visitors and kept in authentic style by the National Park Service. See a park ranger for wedding information.

TEXAS

Just across the river from El Paso, in her sister city *Ciudad Juarez,* stands *la Mission de Nuestra Señora de Guadalupe.* Fray Garcia de San Francisco y Zuñiga built this adobe chapel in 1659, and its four-foot thick walls, tower bell, beams and altar are still wonders of workmanship.

Shop the Mexican markets when planning your wedding here, and you'll find a variety of inexpensive but beautiful peasant gowns for the women in your wedding party and colorful wedding shirts for the groom and his attendants. Buy a bright piñata to fill with sweets and fortunes for a touch of whimsy at the reception, too.

About four miles from the town of *Mission,* Texas, is the quaint *Capilla de la Lomita* (*Chapel of the Hill*). Although it must be reached by farm road 1016 through Madero and then by a short stretch of dirt road, it still offers a sweet wedding site, for it is one of the oldest Texas missions still in use.

UTAH

Pink cliffs and pinnacles offer a colorful and almost unearthly backdrop for an outdoor wedding ceremony of unique proportions when you select *Bryce Canyon* as the site for your ceremony.

The difficult thing about planning a wedding here is that one spot is simply more beautiful than the last. How do you choose between saying your vows under an eons-old natural arch or in front of a towering wind-shaped spire?

Salt Lake City, the home of the Church of Jesus Christ of the Latter-Day Saints, is literally alive with churches of all kinds, each one charming in its own way.

Dominating the possible wedding sites, of course, is the fabu-

lous *Mormon Temple*. To marry here, however, you must be one of Brigham Young's followers of proven faith in good standing, for ceremonies performed in the temple are solemnized not only for this life but for the life hereafter, according to Mormon teachings.

VERMONT

If the wedding guest list is short and the preacher is willing, float your ceremony on the *Fort Ticonderoga Ferry*. There are many trips available from Vermont to New York along Lake Champlain. The trips take from 12 minutes to an hour, so pick one that will at least be long enough to say your I do's and still have time to enjoy some champagne.

You can picture a pretty pilgrim pledging her troth to some smiling Miles Standish in the old *Rockingham Meeting House* two miles northwest of the junction of U.S. 5 and State 103 in Rockingham, Vermont. Here pigpen-style pews erected in 1787 offer a glance back into the days of our founding fathers, for the meeting house is said to be an excellent example of colonial church architecture.

VIRGINIA

"Susan Constant," "Godspeed," and "Discovery," are replicas of the sailing ships that carried the first settlers to Virginia in colonial times. They are moored near *James Fort*, along the *James River*, and offer three distinctly different possibilities for wedding sites. Say your vows standing on their bows or step to the bridge and let the minister stand at the helm as she or he solemnizes your pledge to love one another as long as there are ships and seas.

If you'd have a setting of more conventional mood, try *Trinity Episcopal Church* in *Upperville*. The stone and wood that are used in construction of the 13th-century style church were fashioned by local craftsmen who made their stone cutting tools in a forge right on the site, just as medieval workmen did in Europe. Beautiful sculpture on the pews and windows created in Amsterdam are worthy of note.

WASHINGTON

Claquato Church in *Chehalis* (you get a gold star if you can pronounce both those names right the first time) is one of the oldest religious structures in Washington state. State Highway 6 leads out-of-town about three miles to the church, which boasts a bronze bell cast in Boston in 1857 and shipped around Cape Horn.

If an Oriental theme is in your plans, take to the *University of Washington Arboretum* in *Seattle* for your wedding. There, a Japanese teahouse and authentic Oriental garden offer a sumptuous setting with a Far East flavor.

The garden includes a moon-viewing stand, stone washbasin, and hand-carved granite lanterns.

And if you don't like formal gardens, an Oriental or Western wedding in the Washington woods would be wonderful in dry weather months.

WASHINGTON, D.C.

Just across the Potomac River in *Alexandria, Virginia*, old-fashioned gated pews lend a note of unusual charm to the *Presbyterian Meeting House* on South Fairfax between Wolfe and Duke Streets. Built in 1774, the church is not nearly as famous as its Revolutionary War era burial ground that contains the grave of the unknown soldier from that war. Services are still held here every Sunday at 11 A.M.

East Potomac Park, home of the famous cherry blossoms of *Washington, D.C.,* is an ideal spot for a spring ceremony. In April, 3,000 Japanese cherry trees are in bloom here and around the *Tidal Basin.* There are facilities for picnicking, and boats may be rented. Instead of taking leave of your wedding guests by car, you might rent a boat and sail away from a picnic reception, with guests waving you a happy honeymoon from the shore.

WEST VIRGINIA

Oglebay Park in *Wheeling,* one of the largest municipal parks in the state (1,200 acres), contains gardens, greenhouses, and picnicking areas—all suitable for outdoor weddings in warm weather.

If you're trying to please your mother (or mother-in-law-to-be), why not say your vows in the church where the first Mother's Day observance was held.

Located in *Grafton, Andrews Methodist Church* was the setting for the Mother's Day that started an American tradition way back in 1908.

WISCONSIN

Frank Lloyd Wright designed the *Annunciation Greek Orthodox Church* in *Milwaukee,* at 9400 Congress Street. Incorporating the traditional Byzantine elements of domed roof and Greek cross with its circular components, he created a unique sanctuary which features a blue-tiled dome that rises to a height of 45 feet.

If you want to take an advance look at the facilities, 50 cents will get you in on a guided tour just about any day.

About eight miles outside of *Wisconsin Rapids* on the grounds of *St. Philomena Church* is the *Grotto Shrine,* where a miniature church, sunken gardens, a myriad of artworks and flowers abound.

There is a fee for touring the grotto and wedding arrangements can be discussed with the priest.

WYOMING

Just 2½ miles west of *Lake Junction* in *Yellowstone National Park* is a natural bridge that offers a lovely setting for an al fresco wedding. If this site is not really what you had in mind, head for the Visitor Center for a wealth of other ideas in the country's first national park.

Five Springs Falls, 17 miles east of *Lovell* on U.S. 14-A, offers a splendid recreation area with a number of walk-in wedding sites.

Meet your wedding guests at the campgrounds entrance, then hike to the appointed spot for your ceremony. Let them hike out without you when the knot is tied and you two set up camp for a honeymoon on the spot.

19
bride's checklist
for the big day

On arising (or the night before, if yours is to be a morning wedding):

1. Check weather conditions, in order to make any adjustment in plans that may be affected by inclement weather.
2. Call for the time on the phone (or check with the radio) to make certain your watch is set and everyone involved has the correct time. (You don't want to be late!)
3. Gather together your complete costume and bag it (in a garment bag or cleaner's plastic) for transportation to the church or wherever you'll be dressing.
4. Call attendants and remind them of when and where they are to meet, who is to drive, and so on.
5. Call minister to see if he or she has any last minute requirements.
6. Call organist, soloist, or other musicians you have hired to remind them of the time for set-up or rehearsal.
7. Take a leisurely bath, with lots of perfumed oil, bath foam, or whatever helps you to relax and feel most beautiful.

Midmorning (or four hours before the wedding, at least):

1. Have your hair done, or roll it up if you are doing it yourself.
2. Check your manicure (fingers and toes) and repair as needed.

3. While doing the above, run over your ceremony schedule with your mother and maid of honor, to make sure everyone has been reminded of their duties.

4. Have a light meal or substantial snack. (I've seen brides faint during a long ceremony, not so much from the stress of the joyous occasion, but because they have been too excited to eat beforehand. Don't make this mistake!)

5. Gather together the items in your survival kit to take to the church (hot rollers for fallen curls, nail files, your bridal lipstick, nail polish, comb, brush, hairspray, and so on).

6. Place the survival kit in the car you'll be taking to the church. Do it now! It's easy to forget these vital things in the last-minute rush to get to the church on time. Remember to include a spare pair of pantyhose in case of a run.

7. Take inventory of the flowers. Make sure there are ample corsages, the right number of bouquets, headpieces, and such. It is important to do this while you still have time to correct any mistakes.

Midday:

1. Spend a few minutes alone with each of your parents. A cup of tea with Mom to let her know you appreciate her and an armchair chat with Dad to remind him you're still his little girl will allow you to get any stored-up tears out of the way early.

2. After your private time with your parents, allow youself some quiet time to yourself. Rest or listen to music, to compose yourself before you depart for the ceremony.

3. After your private time, take a brisk shower to refresh yourself.

4. Do your make-up and put on all the jewelry you'll be wearing. Jewelry is easily forgotten if left until you are actually dressing.

An hour before the ceremony:

1. Make certain that everything you'll need at the church is in the car.

2. If you'll be leaving on your honeymoon directly from the reception, make sure your suitcase is packed and in your get-away car.

3. Put final touches on your hair.
4. Repair your make-up, to freshen your overall look.
5. Pose for prewedding photos with bridesmaids.

When the ceremony begins:

1. When you hear the music begin, take a deep breath, hold it for a moment, and exhale slowly.
2. Tuck in your tummy, stand up straight, and *smile!*
3. Walk slowly, making eye contact with friends you see along your way to the altar.

During the ceremony:

1. Speak up! Everyone wants to hear your "I do's."
2. If the tears flow, let them, but keep smiling!
3. Look directly into your partner's eyes as you exchange vows.

After the ceremony:

1. Kiss, but don't linger. It's in bad taste to smooch away in front of the altar. There's a lifetime ahead for that.
2. As you leave the church, acknowledge those you see along the way with a nod, a blown kiss, and so on, and don't hurry down the aisle.
3. Stop on the steps of the church and kiss your partner once more.

At the reception:

1. Even if you've stood in a lengthy reception line, do take time to visit each table and thank your guests for coming.
2. Try to acknowledge gifts that have been received in advance.
3. Most of all . . . *enjoy yourself!*

20
a honey of a . . .
"honeymoon planner!"

Now that you've saved so much money on your wedding, it's time to begin planning the honeymoon of your dreams. And whether you have only time and money for a one night stay or can afford a leisurely trip around the world, there are a few things you can do to insure a honeymoon that will live up to all your little girl dreams.

Although your wedding will be the culmination of many weeks and perhaps months of work, it is not an ending, but a beginning of a whole new life for you and your spouse. So your honeymoon should set the tone for the romantic journey you will take through life together.

Although destination is often the only consideration of couples planning their first days as husband and wife, there are many more important considerations. Just where you honeymoon really isn't all that important. *How* you honeymoon is the key.

So whether you select a secluded mountain cabin or an exotic port of call, consider not only the setting, but also the quality of your surroundings *before* you make your reservations.

It may sound romantic to set off for a two-week sail in a rented sloop, all alone, but unless you're a seasoned sailor and not prone to seasickness, this sort of honeymoon could be a disaster.

Remember, a wedding can be an exhausting experience. You both will have been under a considerable amount of stress in the final days before you become husband and wife, so whatever your honeymoon choices are, seek a plan that will afford you some relaxation, some comfort, and some time to call your own!

Many of the honeymoon packages highly touted by travel agents are tours, and while they are generally less expensive and cover a bit more territory than self-arranged vacations, they often move travelers about on strict schedules that leave little or no time for just kicking back, relaxing, or being spontaneous.

You'll have your whole life to take vacations like that. Let your honeymoon be a time for peace and quiet, romance and intimacy, not rushing and regimentation.

Ask yourselves and your travel agent these questions *first,* before you settle on reservations, destinations, and the like:

1. Will we have the privacy that is so important on a honeymoon?
2. Will we be at the mercy of prearranged schedules?
3. Will inclement weather be a factor in the success or failure of our honeymoon?
4. Will there be ample time for enjoying a spontaneous bit of exploration on our own or just being together, doing nothing if we choose?
5. Will we have the creature comforts we need to be completely at ease and enjoy ourselves?

Even though you both may be avid backpackers or rock climbers, a honeymoon spent scaling Pike's Peak might entail a bit more physical endurance and plain hard work than you'll both be up to. The point is, that whatever choice you make, give yourself a break and let your planning make up for whatever may be missing.

Just a little forethought can turn the most primitive honeymoon plans into a sensuous and exciting experience. But it only takes one important afterthought to turn a dream into a nightmare.

One bride I recall was extremely excited about her fiancé's plan to fly her to Hawaii for an island honeymoon. That is, until the day arrived. She'd been so busy with her wedding plans that she'd actually forgotten her terrible fear of flying until faced with the jumbo jet at the airport.

Her husband had to buy her several stiff drinks and literally "pour her" onto the plane to get her there, and she was so upset by her anxiety during the lengthy flight that her fear of returning occupied much more of her time during their honeymoon than her enjoyment of the orchid-laden lanai room he had reserved for them.

And when the day of departure arrived, no amount of liquor or coaxing could get her to board the plane. So he flew back alone and waited a long ten days for her return by ship. The marriage didn't last long!

If you have any hang-ups, talk them over in advance! Don't hope they will magically vanish the moment he places the ring on your finger. They won't! And this goes for sex, food, allergies, and so on as well as modes of transportation.

Settle on plans that take advantage of your strengths, rather than your weaknesses. And don't keep any important secrets from each other that are likely to be a rude awakening to your partner on your honeymoon. If tropical heat makes your naturally curly hair turn to honeyblonde Brillo, and this bothers you a great deal, let him know, and stay away from the Bahamas, the Mexican jungles, or the South Pacific. You don't want to spend your entire honeymoon trying to get the kinks out of your hair or hiding under a "babushka." Or if he breaks out in a rash every time he eats jalapenos, don't go to Puerto Vallarta.

So, the first step in your honeymoon planning is a good heart-to-heart talk. Once you've got these things out of the way, you can think about the little niceties you'll want to include, things that you can reserve ahead, or take along, that will make any spot a romantic one.

Just as in your wedding, flowers and candles can do a lot to make even the most primitive retreat a honeymoon suite. A thoughtful husband may ask the hotel to send a bouquet to the room, and some hotels, told in advance that the suite will be occupied by newlyweds, will even do this free of charge! But you have to let them know.

Airlines, too, often offer a corsage, or inflight cake for a newly married couple. A bottle of champagne, or the like is often a complimentary item if the airline is just notified at the time the reservations are made.

It is a good idea to call and check this out with the airlines directly, as even good travel agents aren't always aware (and bad ones don't want to be bothered), of these details.

If you are borrowing a beach house, cabin, or even a cabin cruiser for your honeymoon, you'll want to make plans to take flowers and candles along. If you'll have a fireplace, by all means arrange for kindling and logs to make a roaring fire to warm you and inspire your intimacy.

Even if you've lived together for ten years before you decide to marry, your wedding night can be made more memorable by various toiletries, potions, and "sensuousness--essities," you select in advance.

If he has a favorite scent, be sure to stock up on it before you leave. If you love the feel of silk pajamas, splurge and buy him a pair for your honeymoon. If he is wild about girls in garters, but you think they're impractical for everyday wear, surprise him by buying a frilly garter belt or corselette in his favorite shade, even if you feel silly wearing them. Do it once, to please him. The results may surprise you!

There are lots of oils, lotions, bath powders, and other products on the market today that are designed just for the sake of sensuousness. Indulge yourself!

There are even home party plans now that specialize in sexy lingerie, soaps, incredible edibles, and even "toys" that can be fun to experiment with on your honeymoon. And, these are marketed in great part to bachelor parties and nontraditional bridal showers (generally limited to members of the couple's age group only).

The sorority sisters of one friend of mine gave her such a shower, and she set off on her honeymoon with an entire tote filled with "goodies" for each and every day of her honeymoon trip— things like edible body paints, warming heat oils, musky bath bubbles, fruit-flavored lipsticks, lotions, and gels, and even exotic incense and scented candles to burn around the bathtub.

A thoughtful groom of my acquaintance took along a surprise package for his bride that included premixed cocktails (in canned six packs), and lots of little après-sex snacks like caviar, escargot, bite-sized crackers, Cheese Tid-Bits, and her favorite, fresh strawberries! He served them to her in bed, feeding her with his fingers!

And I know one young couple who each provided the other

with a romantic, wrapped present a day, which they exchanged at dinner each night during their honeymoon. They were little things, bought and tucked away in advance during their wedding planning days, but they are treasured mementos of their honeymoon now.

Her gifts to him included a shaving mug, soap and razor (because she liked to watch him shave), a gold-plated toothbrush, an outrageous pair of red bikini shorts, a hand embroidered handkerchief that said, "I love you more each day," and a wallet-sized photo of herself "à la mode," if you get the picture!

His gifts to her were a monogrammed locket with her new initials, a pair of old-fashioned stockings with black seams, an itsy-bitsy pair of baby doll pajamas, a bottle of Heaven Scent, and a tee shirt with the slogan "Very Married!"

These are little fun things that you can do for each other that are sure to add a great deal of excitement and charm to an otherwise ordinary honeymoon. They are inexpensive expressions of your thoughtfulness and love. And they are memories in the making—after all, that's what honeymoons are for.

On the list of "don't forgets" are things you may not find readily available if you are vacationing outside the United States away from urban areas.

It is a good idea to pack a cosmetic case with these essentials a week or two ahead of the wedding and put them in your suitcase early on, while you are unhurried and still thinking clearly. You'll want to make sure you have:

1. Any birth control devices or prescriptions filled and on hand.
2. Any other prescriptions you may need. (Don't forget Dramamine if you're going on a cruise.) Allergy pills, migraine tablets, and so on.
3. Nonprescription drugs, such as Alka-Seltzer, Pepto Bismol (for the dreaded tourista!), aspirin (for the dreaded headache!), Midol, and so on.
4. Toothbrush, mouthwash, toothpaste, razor (disposables are nice), deodorant, shampoo, cream rinse, setting lotion, hairpins, tampons, curlers (a curling wand or electric rollers are a great help), and an extra of your favorite lipstick, blush, and so on.

5. Extra nylons are essential, as pantyhose are a costly item in many places. And you always run your last pair just when you're going out for the most special dinner during your honeymoon.

6. Breath mints and other little candies are also nice to include when traveling, just to refresh you or ward off hunger pangs until room service arrives.

7. And don't forget your passport, airline tickets, or other confirming papers you may need to insure your reservations and travel arrangements. These should go in a separate (plastic so they don't get doused by leaky cosmetics) pouch.

Use the checklist that follows to insure that all the above are packed and neatly tucked away in your luggage long before you'll actually need them. That way, you can rest assured that your honeymoon night won't be spent trying to find an open pharmacy in a strange city because you've left your birth control pills at home on your nightstand.

Many an unexpected visit from the stork has been precipitated by just such carelessness in the crush of wedding day events, and wedding night ardor.

The homecoming is just as much a part of your honeymoon as your wedding reception was, so don't go from glorious newlyweds to old married folks overnight if you can help it.

Be creative! Think ahead and plant a love note beneath your spouse's pillow, before you leave on your honeymoon, or order a bunch of helium balloons delivered and tied to your front door for the day of your return. Little things like this can go a long way toward making your transition from unmarrieds to honeymooners to newlyweds exciting and fun. And they will be completely affordable if you've followed the money-saving wedding plans in this book.

So wherever you go or whatever you do on your honeymoon, do it with love! Do it with a sense of excitement and joy, in a spirit of fun. Make your honeymoon the kind of kick-off to your marriage that will give you lots to look back upon over the years ahead.

And when it's over, consider a repeat performance now and then just for the fun of it. Don't wait for a special occasion to trot out the black stockings he gave you. Don't sit around and hope that he'll remember your fourteenth-week anniversary. Instead, make your whole life together as spontaneous and carefree as a honeymoon could ever be, by keeping the honeymoon spirit alive with the kind of love you are feeling right now.

Express that love in as many ways as possible, using these ideas or dreaming up your own. And if you do, I promise you when problems roll around, as they do in any marriage, the solutions will seem a lot easier.

A honeymoon isn't a place, it's a state of mind. And you have only to travel within yourself to find it and remain there as long as you like, for the rest of your life.

HONEYMOON CHECKLIST

Bride's Checklist

1. Birth control prescriptions or devices
2. Dental needs (toothbrush, paste, mouthwash, and so on)
3. Prescriptions drugs (allergy, sinus, motion sickness)
4. Nonprescription drugs (aspirin, Pepto Bismol, Midol, and so on)
5. Feminine hygiene products (tampons, douche, and so on)
6. Hair products (shampoo, rinse, gel) in travel size
7. Appliances (hot rollers, curling wand, razor, and the like)
8. Toiletries (lotions, oils, bath gel) in travel size
9. Cosmetics (extra lipstick, blush, base, eye makeup)
10. Disposables (nylons, pantyhose, knee-highs, paper goods)
11. Beauty aids (hair brush, comb, mirror, bobbie pins)
12. Goodies (breath mints, Life Savers, gum)
13. Papers (passport, visa, tickets, confirmations)
14. Stationery and pens, stamps
15. Surprises (love potions, toys, and other joys)
16. The_____ he gave me!

Groom's Checklist

1. Shaving gear
2. Birth control aids
3. Dental needs (toothbrush, paste, floss, and so on)

4. Toiletries (after shave, deodorant, cologne)
5. Appliances (hair dryer, electric razor)
6. Prescriptions
7. Traveler's checks
8. Credit cards
9. Foreign currency (if needed)
10. Money belt
11. Autographed copy of "How to Please a Woman"
12. The_____ she gave me!
13. A copy of "How to Please a Man" (for her)
14. Her favorite shirt
15. My favorite (and most comfortable) shoes
16. Flowers for our room (candles too!)
17. A nice little surprise for after sex

21
getting off
to a good start

Tying the knot takes only a few minutes. Keeping it secure can and should be a twenty-four-hour-a-day job for the rest of your life.

But, it doesn't have to be drudgery!

There are many sensational secrets to keeping love alive and keeping a marriage together. The following are some that I've gleaned by polling couples who have been together ten, twenty, thirty, forty years and more.

Some may sound old-fashioned to you. Some silly! Some sentimental and some sublime. All of them may not be for your marriage, but all of them are worth thinking about as you embark upon it.

Why? Because getting off to a good start in a marriage is very important. The first year, as you have probably heard, is the worst. Yet, among the couples I've polled, even with its bumps and starts, its blunders and wonders, most couples look back upon it forever as "the" time to remember, overall.

Here's what they have to say about it—and what to do about it!

Annie and Jack: We fought constantly! But, we kept our senses of humor. Annie learned to draw a smiling face on a piece of paper and tape it to the refrigerator before I came home if she was happy and a sad face if she was sad. Sometimes there was a face with a tongue sticking out at me when I reached inside for a beer. That meant I'd done something to tick her off.

These little signals let me know ahead of time what her mood was, and it helped a lot! Nothing is worse than coming home to a grump when you're in a good mood or the silent treatment when you don't know what's wrong.

Sometimes it's hard to talk about things, but you can give signals, and that's the way we learned to do it. Once she left a skull and cross bones sign. I turned right around, got in the car, and went straight to the florist. She laughed so hard when I came back with a big bouquet that she wouldn't even tell me why she'd been so mad. She said she'd forgotten!

Helen and Frank: The first year we crowded each other something terrible. Frank didn't want me out of his sight. He'd call me three times a day from work. I thought he didn't trust me. It caused a lot of bad situations. And I got suspicious about him.

We settled it after a while by sitting down at night before we went to bed and talking about our plans for the next day. I'd let him know if I was going to be out, and where I planned to go. He'd warn me if he planned to stop anywhere on his way home. It really helped.

Liz and Robert: We went together for five years before we got married. You think you know everything about someone by then. But I found out Robert was a slob! We laugh about it now, but he used to toss his socks in the corner, leave his shorts on the bathroom door, and spread newspapers everywhere. It drove me crazy!

After three months of playing "maid" to him, I got really mad, and for a week I piled up everything he'd dropped on the floor on his side of the bed. Each night before he got in bed, he'd have to clear it all away. He got the hint. Now his socks go in the hamper and the paper in the trash—and when he slips up, I don't mind picking up occasionally, if I know he's in a rush.

Bill and Jo Ann: It seems like Jo Ann cried for the whole first year of our marriage. She wouldn't fight! When she got angry, she'd go in the bedroom and slam the door and cry. Half the time I didn't even know what was wrong. And she couldn't tell me.

One day I got smart and slipped a note under the door. It was just a blank piece of paper that said, "I know I'm a heel but I don't know why. I'll try to be better if you'll give me a list of things to work on." And I numbered the rest of the lines on the page, from 1 to 25. She could only think of three things to fill in, and it made her feel foolish.

Since then we make lists of good and bad deeds done, and each of us tries to respond by working on them. After 28 years we still do it.

Linda and George: We were poor! And, we both wanted things we couldn't afford yet. We fought about money all the time. After 15 years it's still our number one problem, but we've learned to save for special things. Here's how we do it. I took two big mayonnaise jars and labeled them his and hers. Each day, we'd drop our change into them. When they were full we each opened our own savings account, separate from our joint accounts. If I want an expensive pair of boots, that's the fund I use to buy them. If he wants a power tool, he dips into his "mayonnaise." We still can't afford all the goodies we'd like, but neither of us is jealous when the other has saved enough to get something special for himself.

Jim and Dorothy: Before we were married we went out a lot. The first year it seemed we never left the apartment. It was partly because of finances and partly because we thought married people were supposed to stay home. But we both hated it! After a huge row I screamed at Jim, "I want to date. I want to go out and have fun! I hate being married!"

He laughed. Then, he asked me for a date. And, ever since we go out once a week at least. Friday night is date night, and we do a lot of the same things we did before we got married. We take in a movie, have dinner out (even if it's just hamburgers), see a play, or go dancing. We both look forward to it.

Over the years, we've added little vacations to this plan, mini-honeymoons. Three or four times a year we take off for a night in a motel, a weekend away, or a holiday weekend.

There's something really sensuous about sneaking off to a motel right in town and just spending the night in a strange bed. And it doesn't cost much more than dinner and a movie.

Our "dates" have saved our marriage a hundred times. Sometimes after we've had a tiff, Jim will leave the house, check into a motel, and call me. He'll say, "I can stay here till you cool off or you can join me. He's never stayed alone! It's his way of making up, and I love it!

Carole and Lee: This is going to sound strange, but neither of us really felt married until we started having friends over for dinner. Somehow, we acted like roommates. Single people living together. We both worked. We shared expenses. We got along okay, but we didn't feel like a "couple." It took our first dinner party for him to see me as his wife, and appreciate me. And I really enjoyed the way he pitched in to prepare and clean up afterwards. So now when I feel unappreciated, I ask him to invite friends in. He gets the message. We work together to make a party, and it usually winds up with us feeling more together later.

Jan and Tom: Our expectations were out of sync! I wanted champagne and flowers, and he expected meatloaf and potatoes. We almost called it quits after six months. But, in a rage one night, I heard each of us saying, "I expected," and "I thought," and "you're supposed to" enough to see things more clearly.

The next day we sat down and shared our expectations and the realities. Now we have a kind of understanding. We only fight about what has actually happened, not what we thought, hoped, or wanted to happen. It's worked for us.

Jenny and Paul: I'm an artist, and Paul is an accountant. He loves his work and so do I, but each of us was jealous of the other's extra time spent on these things.

Paul considered his work, because it paid the rent, more important than mine, which was strictly for pleasure. It was okay for him to spend endless hours at the office, but not for me to paint while he was home. He wanted to be my hobby as well as my husband. I wanted to be as important as his work.

We were in conflict over this for our first three years of marriage. We finally solved this problem by deciding on a night off routine. Rather than spending an extra hour or two at the office every night, Paul comes home on time four nights a week and cleans up his left over work every Thursday night. Now I know I have Thursday to paint to my heart's content. We're both more productive, and the other evenings we are eager to be together, not thinking of an unfinished project we'd like to be working on.

Like these couples, you will have sore points in your marriage that need working out. Their solutions may not be the right ones for you, but you can consider them.

And you may want to consider the hints that follow, as well. These were among the most often suggested by respondents to my happy marriage survey.

1. *Never go to bed angry.* Try to work out any differences before you climb between the sheets.

2. *Learn to laugh at yourself.* If you burn the pot roast, call it "Pot Roast à la Smokey Bear." A little humor works wonders.

3. *Give in just for the joy of it!* If you want to go to a movie and he wants to go to a hockey game, give in without a fuss now and then. You'll find he'll learn to do likewise sooner or later.

4. *Forgive your partner and yourself.* When someone has hurt you or you have struck out in anger, forgive. Forget. And, don't let guilt get you down. Neither of you is perfect. Be sorry but don't be guilty. And, don't bring it up again, *ever!*

5. *Be spontaneous.* Many marriages die of boredom. Don't let that happen to yours. Surprise your spouse now and then, with a note on the mirror, in his lunch, a small gift, or a special treat for no special occasion.

6. *Think before you speak.* Words are weapons; they can hurt deeply. Do your best to spend your words as wisely as you spend your money. Choose them carefully, and let your partner know exactly how you feel, but think it over yourself first.

7. *Remember the good times.* When things are going wrong, bring up a time when things were perfect and talk about that. Let your spouse know you remember, and he or she will remember too.

8. *Ask for advice.* Independence is great, and every marriage needs a large dose of it on both sides. But let your spouse know you value his or her advice. Ask for input. Give your mate a chance to make a suggestion or give you encouragement.

9. *Be a friend.* Many husbands and wives are more considerate of their family and friends than they are of each other. Think of your mate as a friend if you want him or her to be one. Call just to say hello. Send a card for fun. Remember things that count, like wearing gifts you've received, making a favorite meal, and so on. You'd do that for a friend, wouldn't you?

10. *Say "I Love You" every day.* Come right out and say it! Don't expect your partner to know you care. Tell him or her, often.

12. *Touch each other.* Don't stop holding hands once you've exchanged wedding bands. Hug! Kiss! Make contact! Science has proven that without touching, we lose that lovin' feeling. Keep it alive. We need at least three hugs a day, just to survive.

13. *Respect his/her privacy.* Everyone needs some time alone. Some time to think, or read, or putter around. Don't intrude on this time. Don't pry or ask too many questions about it. Give it as a gift of love. The rewards are amazing.

14. *Make your mate proud.* Whatever you do, do your very best. Give your partner something to tell your friends about. Try to excel at something that pleases him or her. Your accomplishments are a big contribution to your marriage.

15. *Experiment.* Try things you've never tried before. Listen for clues to things your partner might like or be interested in, and surprise him/her by giving them a try.

16. *Be honest.* Little lies can often become big ones. Don't do something you wouldn't want your mate to find out about. And, better yet, don't do anything you wouldn't tell him or her about yourself.

17. *Play fair.* Don't ask for favors you aren't willing to return. Don't expect your mate to sacrifice for things you want unless you would do the same.

18. *Put the marriage before the carriage.* Children can come between parents, but only if you let them. You'll be doing your children a favor if you let them know your love started with your mate and extends to them. And your mate will feel secure to do the same.

19. *Live in the now.* Don't let things that happened in the past spoil today. Don't let what you're hoping for tomorrow keep you from enjoying the present. Spend each day of your married life as if it were your last dollar, wisely, on important things. All your tomorrows will take care of themselves.

Marriage is an adventure. From planning your wedding and honeymoon, to your retirement, marriage is to enjoy. Work together from the start to make each moment of your life as special, as exciting, as much fun as the anticipation of your wedding day.

Learn and grow with each new experience. Share and care for one another always, as you do right now. Believe in the dream you have now, and believe it or not, it will come true.

index